TOTALLY SCRIPTED

IDIOMS, WORDS, AND QUOTES
FROM HOLLYWOOD
TO BROADWAY
THAT HAVE CHANGED
THE ENGLISH LANGUAGE

JOSH CHETWYND

Guilford, Connecticut

An imprint of Globe Pequot
Distributed by NATIONAL BOOK NETWORK

British Library Cataloguing in Publication Information Available

Library of Congress Cataloging-in-Publication Data Available

ISBN 978-1-63076-282-7
ISBN 978-1-63076-283-4 (e-book)

∞™ The paper used in this publication meets the minimum requirements of American
National Standard for Information Sciences—Permanence of Paper for Printed Library
Materials, ANSI/NISO Z39.48-1992.

Printed in the United States of America

For my Oscar-worthy wife and children:
Jennifer, Miller, and Becca

CONTENTS

INTRODUCTION

Show business has always understood the value of words. Whether on the silver screen, television, radio, or stage, how a film, program, or play is written is crucial to a production's success or failure. "You struggle, you claw, and you scratch trying to camouflage a bad script," beloved actor Gregory Peck once said. "When the script is sound and the structure is there, you just sort of sail through."

Behind the scenes the specificity of what's said is every bit as important. When a late nineteenth-century stagehand was told to make sure the star was *in the limelight*, he'd be in big trouble if he didn't know how to make that happen. (For more on limelight go to p. 91.) Similarly, a film editor in the early days of Hollywood would lose his job if he didn't understand how to deftly *cut to the chase* (p. 54).

Then there are the many studio execs, talent agents, and publicists who have intuitively understood how to bend language to their will since the dawn of the business. As an entertainment journalist for publications like *USA Today* and the *Hollywood Reporter*, I've often quipped that there are certain power players in the industry who like to lie with moral indignation. If you question what seems like a tall tale, these Hollywood bigwigs become outraged. It's as if they are saying, "How dare you question my lie? Do you know who I am? You should consider yourself lucky that I'm even lying to you!"

For better or for worse, this book celebrates how all these elements have led to show business making such a lasting impact on what we say every day.

In 2016 the *Economist* magazine explained why it was relaunching a column on language in its print edition: "Its power to inform and to lead astray, to entertain and to annoy, to build co-operation or destroy reputation, makes language serious stuff." In the hands of the dream factories that produce movies, television, radio, and theater, all those factors are not only in play, but, to paraphrase the film *This Is Spinal Tap*, they also generally go to eleven on a scale of one to ten.

The reason: Everything is bigger in showbiz. Culture is America's largest export, and what takes place in that industry is so often at the center of what is being sold. So when movie censors in the 1940s decided that an obscure word primarily used in geology would become the term for that often-ogled top part of a woman's chest, the little-used *cleavage* got a new meaning and went global almost instantly. Or when Arnold Schwarzenegger warned "I'll be back" in *The Terminator*, you could quickly find posters, T-shirts, and mugs all for sale with that catchphrase (not to mention an ungodly number of newspaper headlines later when the actor ran for and then served as California's governor). Quite simply, what happens in Hollywood does *not* stay in Hollywood.

With that in mind, what should you expect in these pages? This book delves into how the entertainment universe has transformed the English language through idioms, words, and quotes. So what you'll find here are the stories behind why phrases from *ad-libbing* to *wing it* are no longer solely the domain of the thespian world. Moreover, explanations for everything from why losing your job can be described as *getting the hook* to the background on how calling a person a *drama queen* transitioned from being a compliment to an insult are covered.

That said, entertainment industry phrases that haven't developed into figurative mainstays in common conversation are sidestepped here. For example, there's some great movie jargon out there. Among my favorites are terms like *best boy*, which is the name for the number-two person in a movie production's electrical department, and a *gobo*, which is slang for an object used to block an unwelcomed light during shooting. Sadly, as much as I'd like to see somebody say, "get a *gobo* for that lamp" when you're trying to go to bed, it didn't make the cut because it hasn't gained that broader appeal.

Along with the main entries, you'll also find a lot of space devoted to the history of iconic film quotes. It was a no-brainer to include them. After all, as the *Los Angeles Times* said in 2010: "If music is the soundtrack of our lives, then movies provide the audio track." Still, this was a challenging aspect to the book as, for most of us, a great movie line evokes a very personal time and place in our lives.

As a result, I held my breath as I chose thirty great lines of dialogue for inclusion. How did I pick them? I looked for examples that are often at the tips of our tongues, stood out in film history, and also provided interesting *backstories* (see p. 7 for that term's, well, backstory). In making my selections I was primarily guided by two sources: A list generated by the American Film Institute in 2005 called "AFI's 100 Years . . . 100 Movie Quotes" and a 2016 survey of industry pros conducted by the *Hollywood Reporter* dubbed "Hollywood's 100 Favorite Movie Quotes." Oh, and for you TV fans, fear not: There is space devoted to quotes from that medium as well (see pp. 36, 111, and 187).

To steal a saying from TV commercials, "But wait, there's more!" This work also features other boxes and lists illustrating how in many ways, big and small, all sorts of showbiz folks have left their mark on the lexicon.

A couple of final points before we get rolling. First, the book aims to be a robust survey of this topic rather than an exhaustive tome. The hope is that I've touched on a broad range of words and phrases taken from the entertainment industry that we now ordinarily use. But if I've neglected a few, apologies. Nevertheless, before you have a *prima donna* (p. 133) moment, consider perusing the index as some idioms may be discussed as part of other entries. Finally, I always aim to give credit where credit is due, so if you're looking for detailed sourcing for any quotes that appear in this book, please check the notes section.

Now, in honor of the longtime Loews Theatres' jingle, I hope you'll sit back and relax, (and) enjoy the book.

IDIOMS, WORDS, AND QUOTES

Ad-libbing

The popularity of *ad-libbing*—whether you're unprepared and need to give a presentation at work or you're trying to talk your way out of a parking ticket—came in large part from the dramatic arts.

However, the music world deserves initial paternity. The expression comes from the musical notation *ad lib.*, which is short for *ad libitum*, meaning "at one's pleasure or discretion," according to the *Oxford English Dictionary*. In the 1700s, when *ad lib.* was added to a musical score, it told the conductor he had the option to use a certain instrument in a performance.

In the 1800s both stage and music took the phrase to describe improvisation. Still, a big breakthrough for the term came in the early decades of the 1900s, when theater and film folks began commonly using it as a verb (as in *ad-libbing* or *ad-libbed*) to express on-the-fly changes to dialogue and action.

At that time newspapers like the *New York Times* treated the expression as if it were something completely new—though even the paper of record wasn't completely sure what it meant. In a 1926 article the *Times* defined *ad-libbing* on the stage as "spoofing, joshing, mocking, or plain unembroidered kidding."

By 1929 the often-described newspaper of record had a better grip on the term when it ran a feature on how the new art of talking films often needed *ad-libbing* for technical purposes. Sound engineers required this additional impromptu conversation, which the article defined as "improvised dialogue," to create continuity in the soundtrack.

During this era, when an actor was good at this practice, it became worthy of media attention. The *Washington Post* ran its own 1929 story about how great actors were *ad-libbing* their way through films. The best, according to the paper, was Will Rogers. In the movie *They Had to See Paris*, the paper gushed that the comic actor "ad libbed enough of his dialogue to have his role truly 'all Rogers.'"

No doubt, music has continued to use the phrase (heck, it's a foundation for the American art form of jazz), but the early movie references, which were far more common in newspapers than musical mentions at this point, solidified the expression as commonplace in the English language.

To be sure, the practice has remained central in filmmaking ever since. Beyond the *ad-libbed* movie quotes discussed in full in these pages (see: "Here's looking at you, kid," "You talkin' to me?" and "You're going to need a bigger boat" as examples on pages 28, 176, and 182, respectively), other great improvised lines in pictures include: Dustin Hoffman's street-crossing statement in *Midnight Cowboy*, "Hey, I'm walkin' here!"; the iconic line "squeal like a pig" from *Deliverance*; and Jack Nicholson's über-creepy "*Heeeerrrreeee's* Johnny!" in *The Shining*.

Audition

Most actors will tell you that almost invariably, *auditions* have a meat-market quality to them. It's more about how you look than what you say. If that's the case, then those hiring are generally missing the actual meaning of *audition*. English speakers first took the word in the sixteenth century to describe the act of hearing. For instance, doctors would talk about the *audition* of a patient (e.g., the deaf man lacks *audition*).

But by the 1800s the French were also using the term regularly for a broader purpose. An *audition* was used to label a hearing in court. For example, French legal code would talk about *l'audition des témoins*, which were hearings of witnesses. This idea of having your moment to speak in front of important individuals was taken by theater operators by the 1870s. An early reference to the crossover can be found in the August 1879 edition of *Theatre* magazine, when it discussed how an actor "applied for an audition" with the Comédie Française.

At the start of the twentieth century, actors on both sides of the Atlantic were formally lining up for *auditions* (aka tryouts)—often much to the chagrin of all involved.

In 1912 movie mogul Adolph Zukor hired pioneering filmmaker Edwin S. Porter to produce six films. Porter, who likely chafed at the *auditioning* required for that number of projects, supposedly remarked, "There isn't that much talent in the world."

More than ninety years later, in 2003, Robert De Niro gave his perspective on his early experiences with the process.

"I didn't have a problem with rejection, because when you go into an audition, you're rejected already," he said. "There are hundreds of other actors. You're behind the eight ball when you go in there."

Indeed, the numbers of people who are tested for a single part can seem exhaustive. *General Hospital* casting director Mark Teschner once said he'd read 250 actors for a single role, but that's nothing compared to the thousands upon thousands who auditioned to become iconic characters like Harry Potter or *Gone with the Wind*'s Scarlett O'Hara.

Still, there are rare instances when a soft side to it all emerges. For the movie *Mystic Pizza*, Julia Roberts originally came in to *audition* unprepared. She reportedly hadn't read the script, wasn't dressed right, and, with blond hair, didn't look the part. Rather than dismiss her, the casting directors told Roberts what they wanted and asked her to come back the next day. This time Roberts had colored her hair, was wearing the appropriate clothes, and had prepared her lines. She nailed it and got what would be a breakout role.

> ## "All right, Mr. DeMille,
> I'm ready for my close-up."
> —Norma Desmond (Gloria Swanson),
> *Sunset Boulevard* (1950)

When you pull back the curtain on how *Sunset Boulevard* came together, you begin to realize how easily the movie—and this quote—could have been vastly different.

Billy Wilder and his longtime writing partner Charlie Brackett collaborated with D. M. Marshman Jr. on the project. The original idea was to tentatively call it *A Can of Beans* and make it about a "harassed head of the studio, half heavy, half hero, who dies of heat exhaustion driving back from a [movie] preview in Pomona [California]," Brackett confided in his diary.

They ditched that premise and, in the end, Wilder was motivated by something he'd jotted down some time before. The filmmaker kept a log of promising ideas he'd come up with over the years. "When he consulted his notebook," wrote biographer Gene Phillips (spoiler alert!), "he found this fragment: 'Silent picture star commits murder. When they arrest her, she sees the newsreel cameras and thinks she is back in the movies.'"

With that discovery, the foundation was cemented for this line, which served as the film's final words. But the picture still almost went in a completely different direction for another reason. "God forgive me, I wanted to have Mae West" play faded silent movie star Norma Desmond, Wilder once admitted.

West would have surely interpreted the role—and this line—with her trademark bawdy demeanor, making the picture more of a comedy than a satirically dark tale. Sam Staggs, who wrote a history of the film, mused that "from Mae's mouth, 'I'm ready for my close-up' wouldn't be addressed to DeMille but to a young stud and she'd make it clear she didn't mean a camera shot."

Wilder and West both agreed she wasn't right for the part, and while some other actresses, like Mary Pickford, were discussed, the marriage of the onetime silent film star Gloria Swanson and the role proved a perfect match.

When it came to this scene, which the writers were still fine-tuning well after shooting began, Swanson was an absolute ace. In particular, Brackett was impressed by her "fantastic stamina" in filming it.

She's "a woman of fifty who spent the day going down a staircase without looking at the steps, having her hands in a strange Salome-esque dance fashion, who at eight o'clock had to do her most highly emotional scene, and who seemed to get through with no bad effects whatever," he wrote in his diary. After Swanson uttered the famous lines for the final time (this also happened to be the last scene she shot in the film), the crew burst into applause.

Sunset Boulevard was also the end of a relationship between Wilder and Brackett that had spanned seventeen screenplays and earned two Academy Awards (including one for this film). The duo certainly went out on top as a team. Along with this line, Desmond's statement "I am big! It's the pictures that got small" is also deemed one of the most memorable in film history. ★

Backdrop

Compared to their British counterparts, Americans have long enjoyed simplifying the English language. The Brits fill their cars with *petrol* while Yanks use *gas*. In the United States, people often eat *eggplant*, which is called *aubergine* in the United Kingdom. If it's raining outside, a guy in Seattle will put on his *rain boots*; a similar fellow in London will reach for his *Wellingtons*.

With that in mind, maybe it should come as no surprise that in the late nineteenth century, American theater pros came up with the plainer *backdrop*—rather than the British-used *scenery*—to describe those beautifully painted background canvases that depicted a show's location.

The term was certainly popular in New York, where newspapers were referring to *backdrops* by the 1890s. Nonetheless, it's probably much older than that. A story that ran in small papers throughout the Midwest in 1893 talked about how a theater "manager fell against the back-drop" without needing any explanation of what that object might be.

Before the 1900s the seeds of the word's metaphorical use were already planted. In September 1899 a syndicated article about the triumphant return of Admiral George Dewey to New York after fighting in the Philippines was front-page news in big newspapers like Atlanta's *Constitution* and the *Salt Lake City Tribune*.

The widely circulated story described the scene as Dewey journeyed through the city saying, "Stores, old office buildings, and modern scrapers were crowded with stands, tiers upon tiers of seats like an immense theater, whose roof was the sky, whose walls were the surrounding hills, and whose back-drop was the horizon of the lower bay."

Since then, the word has been used—often in the construction *against the backdrop*—to set the context for everything from great moments in history to the stakes in an upcoming football game.

While the word has risen in stature, those who actually create backdrops haven't. Back in 1891 the *New York Times* would give shout-outs to "scene painters" in its columns.

Today, backdrop artists have generally lost that rock-star status. Still, that doesn't mean they haven't continued to do great work through the years. For example, it took twenty artists to create a *backdrop* that served as a crossroads on the yellow brick road in *The Wizard of Oz*. While their names aren't necessarily remembered, this group expertly painted a 400-foot-long and 35-foot-high piece of heavy white muslin in the vivid colors of the world of Oz.

Backstory

The backstory behind *backstory* is relatively short. One of the first examples of this expression (often written as *back story*) for a background narrative can be found in the 1970s as a television writing device—though it was probably used in the film business as well.

In a 1976 *New York Times* feature on the soap opera *Ryan's Hope*, the term was mentioned in quotes, suggesting it was a novelty to the reader at the time. Before the daytime drama debuted in 1975, the actors got "themselves up for the task by means of a 100-page 'back story,'" the article said. Conceptually, this early version of a *backstory* was deep. "This [*backstory*] book is a genealogy of the TV characters going back to the turn-of-the-century arrival of the immigrant Ryan family, a book full of details, traits and whole ancestors that were mere prologue," the article explained.

Oh, how times have changed. By 1986 the phrase evolved to also describe real people's backgrounds, and while our modern use of *backstory* sometimes has depth, it often shows up in conjunction with quick-hit portraits of the past.

For example, a journalist in 2006 boiled down the "back story of the Christmas narrative" to "a story about fragile families, poverty and the good community."

The *New York Times Magazine* took *backstory* as a heading on its contents page for a similar cursory glance. "What we mean to do in that paragraph is give you a little 'back story' on the author—why he

Continued on p. 10

> ## "Fasten your seat belts, it's going to be a bumpy night."
> ## —Margo Channing (Bette Davis), *All About Eve* (1950)

All About Eve is widely regarded as one of writer-director Joseph L. Mankiewicz's master classes in screenwriting. Along with this piece of dialogue, Mankiewicz, who won his second Best Screenplay Oscar for this work, offered scores of zingers.

They included (but weren't limited to): "I wouldn't worry too much about your heart. You can always put that award where your heart ought to be"; "You're too short for that gesture"; "Miss Caswell is an actress, a graduate of the Copacabana School of the Dramatic Arts"; and "Funny business, a woman's career. The things you drop on your way up the ladder so you can move faster. You forget you'll need them again when you get back to being a woman."

But this line stands out because of how, in particular, Bette Davis interpreted it from the page.

"Fasten your seat belts, it's going to be a bumpy night" came to Mankiewicz very early on. He had it in his first treatment, which is essentially an initial detailed outline. When the shooting script was completed, the line didn't include any direction other than to have Davis's diva Margo Channing respond to a question from her friend Karen Richards (played by Celeste Holm), who wondered whether Channing was about to create a scene.

Instead, Davis did some physical improvisation, downing her martini and swaggering around before delivering the famous words with tart satisfaction.

"Those are things you should be able to do as an actress that a director wouldn't think of telling you," Davis said about her additions. "When Margo holds back like that, it lets you know she's collecting more venom."

What's astonishing is that while Davis's work—and line—in this movie were deemed signature performances, she wasn't booked for the role until nearly the last minute. Claudette Colbert had been signed to play Margo but had to drop out because of a back injury. While others like Marlene Dietrich and Gertrude Lawrence were considered, Davis got the job.

Mankiewicz would say a year before his death in 1993 that the switch from Colbert to Davis made all the difference for this iconic statement. In fact, he actually once asked Colbert to recite the famous words sometime after the film came out.

He said Colbert delivered it in a "darling" fashion, but it didn't capture the mood like Davis had done. Davis said it perfectly, according to Mankiewicz, like she was "hoisting storm warnings."

Davis's cautionary statement certainly cottoned to the minds of audiences—maybe a little too much, according to longtime *New York Times* film critic Vincent Canby.

"The line has now been so thoroughly absorbed into the collective subconscious that many people no longer remember its origins," Canby wrote in 1992. "It [has] passed into the public domain, better recognized as the happy hunting ground where one man's wit gains immortality as another man's cliché." ★

or she was the one to have reported and written the piece," Gerald Marzorati, editor of the magazine, said in 2005.

Although *backstories* are often reductive, they are nevertheless considered important for everybody and everything. In 2007 the *Washington Post* talked about how Barack Obama knew he needed to possess "both a cause and a back story." The same paper lauded a theater group seven years later for its portrayal of "the back story behind our impossible-to-sing national anthem."

As far as its linguistic staying power, *backstory* may just be one of those terms that has a particularly memorable quality. "We at the magazine use it on our contents page mostly because of the catchiness of the phrase," Marzorati explained.

Behind the scenes

Behind the scenes of any production is a complicated place.

"Nearly all people who ever visit the opera or theatre . . . [know] there is a dark mysterious space behind the scene, where the artists move about," an 1874 *Harper's* magazine article said. "But very few have a conception—even the faintest—of the immensity of these secret regions compared with the stage upon which their eyes rest when the curtain is up."

While not discussing behind the stage, per se, the article described how major theaters possessed three or four distinct stories below where the actors tread. Before our modern-day mechanics, some of the intricate contraptions necessary to move thespians onto the stage from below or shift scenery could fill up a whole subterranean floor or more.

In the film world, *behind the scenes* is no less intricate. Take MGM during the golden age of 1930s moviemaking. The studio boasted 3,200 artisans, laborers, technicians, and craftsmen on staff. That included five hundred carpenters, fifteen plumbers, twenty-four guys in the blacksmith shop, and even a barber.

Despite all those toiling away in obscurity, the phrase doesn't appear to have been originally coined to describe their work. Instead, it was a term of art to reflect activities performed by characters outside the view of the audience—like an offstage birth or murder.

The playwright John Dryden used it way back in 1668 when he wrote: "But there is another [s]ort of Relations, that is, of things happening in the Action of the Play, and [s]uppos'd to be done behind the Scenes."

Even so, the expression quickly found broader meaning both on the stage and in the general vernacular. Before the end of the seventeenth century, it was applied figuratively for anything (in the theater or otherwise) done away from public scrutiny.

Not surprisingly, with that meaning came a desire to keep people away from these private activities. As a 1701 London newspaper fumed about the goings-on at one theater: "Many Noblemen and Gentlemen Observing how Shamefully the Players are Impos'd upon by a great many Persons who come into the Side Boxes and behind the Scenes, and never Pay any thing for seeing the Play."

More than three centuries later, *behind the scenes* (or, as some like to call it, *backstage*, which became a popular idiom in the twentieth century) remains a touchy place—particularly in the world of politics. In 2008 Australia's Health Minister, Nicola Roxon, admitted that the backroom business of spinning journalists wasn't pretty.

"Our handling of the media is a bit like sausage making: Some things you don't want to see behind the scenes," she said.

The big picture

If you want to use show business as your guide, figuring out *the big picture* in life should be less about securing a sky-high overview of a problem or situation and more about getting a quality perspective.

While the phrase *big picture* as a literal description of a large painting has been around for a long time, this expression found its

Continued on p. 14

"Frankly my dear, I don't give a damn."
—Rhett Butler (Clark Gable),
Gone with the Wind (1939)

In 2005 the American Film Institute named these unforgettable parting words the greatest movie quote of all time. But would the line have been as meaningful if, instead, Rhett had said, "Frankly, my dear, I don't care" or "Frankly, my dear, I don't give a hoot"?

Both were on the table in the months leading up to *Gone with the Wind*'s December 1939 premiere. In the early days of the movie business, Hollywood was pretty lax about language, but in 1930 a more conservative Motion Picture Association instituted a Production Code, known as the Hays Code, that outlawed many things (see *Cleavage*, p. 40), including a number of words deemed racy, like "damn."

But David O. Selznick, who produced the eventual Best Picture Oscar winner, would not be denied. Though he replaced the iconic line with "Frankly, my dear, I don't care" at a screening for censors, he had a bigger plan. That version got the regulators' seal of approval, which was necessary for the film to be distributed, and then the producer really went to work.

He wrote a lengthy letter to the code's chieftain Will Hays, arguing "damn" be reinstated. He noted that numerous upstanding magazines of the day, like the *Saturday Evening Post* and the *Atlantic Monthly*, featured the word, and that the line had literary basis. Margaret Mitchell had used the almost identical phrase "My dear, I don't give a damn" in her book, which won the Pulitzer Prize for Fiction in 1937.

"The omission of this line spoils the punch at the very end of the picture," Selznick wrote, "and on our very fade-out gives an impression of unfaithfulness after three hours and forty-five minutes of extreme fidelity to Miss Mitchell's work which has become . . . an American Bible."

Hays and his office were unmoved, so the backroom drama was ratcheted up. On October 27 a meeting with the Board of Directors of the Motion Picture and Producers Distribution Association was held to discuss the line. The confab was described to Selznick, who didn't attend the gathering, as "a very stormy session."

Nevertheless, Selznick got his way. The code was quietly modified on November 1 to allow elements "essential and required for portrayal, in proper historical context, of any scene or dialogue based upon historical fact or folklore . . . or a quotation from a literary work, provided that no such use shall be permitted which is intrinsically objectionable or offends good nature." The movie's final line met that requirement.

Despite the victory, a legend exists that the producer was still fined $5,000 for using "damn." There is no known evidence in Selznick's or the production code's archives to support that ever happened. In the end the often-repeated tale might have simply been a myth created to protect the Hays Office from embarrassment for yielding on this issue.

Still, in view of the film's ultimate success, if Selznick did indeed make a payment, you can be sure his first thought was: "Frankly my dear, I don't give a damn." ★

way into show business during the first few decades of the twentieth century—just before the idiomatic usage became particularly popular. But rather than being used to express the size of movie screens, it was initially applied to stage productions, and then, more regularly, to films that were touted as the prime product.

For instance, a February 1904 issue of the *Evening News Review* in East Liverpool, Ohio, gushed that the final act of a musical called *While Old Glory Waves* was the "big picture" of the proceedings. By the next decade, publications were commonly utilizing the term either to generally reference feature films (as opposed to short movies) or to describe a major, big-budget production. (An example from a January 1916 edition of the *Bakersfield Californian*: "The vaudeville and the Pathe News Review will precede the big picture, starting at 7 o'clock sharp.") In addition, a "big picture house" was often used to describe an establishment that showed these higher-production full-length films.

With this usage very much in play during the 1930s, when folks began using *big picture* figuratively, it's possible it served as inspiration for the idiomatic phrase. Still, it's hard to deny that the literal big screens that moviegoers were experiencing didn't have an impact as that application certainly suggests taking a wide view on a subject.

Without question, early screens were impressive spectacles for the time. Original large cinemas, for example, could boast screens that measured up to 24 by 18 feet. Of course, that's nothing compared to today's massive options like the IMAX viewing surface at Darling Harbour in Sydney, Australia, which is a jaw-dropping 117 by 97 feet.

Still, even though pioneering screens are not as awe-inspiring as today's standards, you could be sure you'd get an up-close-and-personal view in those older theaters—a fact that wasn't lost on the actors being displayed.

Joked comedic actor Joe E. Brown, who made his film debut in 1928: "When I first saw my face on the screen in a close-up six feet high, I jumped up and yelled, 'It's a lie!'"

Bit part

A *bit*, which originally entered the English language to describe a morsel of food, is an ancient word that comes from the idea of biting. But when we talk about a *bit part* in any sort of activity, forget about eating. It comes from showbiz.

On second thought, don't completely forget about eating, as having a small enough role to be deemed a *bit player* means making so little money it might be tough to both buy groceries and pay the rent. In 1926 a regular bit role in a Broadway production would get you a meager $20 a week, which is about $267 in modern terms. Today, an actor who has five lines or less on a 30-minute TV series earns a minimum of $401 for a one-day role.

Even worse, taking a *bit part* means more than just not having much face time in the show. It's also an implicit reminder that, in general, you aren't big-time. That's because around the same time a *bit part* became common stage jargon in the 1920s, another expression, *cameo*, emerged.

That word was used for a small role reserved for actors of substantial stature. In 1956 the Oscar-winning *Around the World in 80 Days* really popularized the usage of *cameo* when it boasted forty-six such performances from greats such as Marlene Dietrich, Frank Sinatra, Buster Keaton, and Red Skelton. The takeaway is if you have a few lines and you aren't getting the *cameo* moniker, you probably aren't highly regarded.

Nevertheless, there are upsides to taking a measly part. Most notably, it's long been a stepping stone. Even back in 1925 the successful director and studio exec Monta Bell told a reporter that he hired journeyman actor Charlie McHugh for a large role in the Marion Davies vehicle *Lights of Old Broadway* primarily because the actor was willing to take a "bit part" in a previous film.

Glory can also come to these briefly seen and heard players. Beatrice Straight is the prime example. The lesser-known performer won a supporting actress Oscar for a mere five minutes and forty seconds of screen time in the 1976 film "Network," which ran a total of 121 minutes.

Language-wise, the role of the bit player hasn't been solely the domain of actors for decades. *Bit parts*, at least according to the media, really run the gamut from football players to, if you can believe it, the pope. Of course, like most actors, elected officials, in particular, strive to avoid the tag. "Politicians don't come to Washington to play a bit part in the opera," explained one newspaper in 2015.

Blackout

As the film *The Hangover* (just the original, not the sequels) proves, *blackouts* can be entertaining. Although if you've ever had your own bender that's led to such an experience, it's certainly more drama than comedy.

While we can't credit the theater for the creation of those experiences, we can say it brought the term *blackout* to light. The word was initially stage jargon for extinguishing all lights in a performance. Think of it as the cinematic version of a *fade-out* (see p. 63). This immediate darkness was done for various purposes—to mark the end of a scene, the passage of time, a particularly compelling moment, or, in other instances, to indicate that the show was shifting from one vaudeville act to another.

This terminology was very much in use during the first decades of the 1900s. The illustrious playwright George Bernard Shaw made reference to it in a letter he penned in 1913. Still, it should be said that this thematic strategy was not always welcomed. Its use in a 1928 London production led a critic for the *Times* of London to ask whether the tactic was a simplistic dramatic crutch. "Is the mere dropping of a gauze curtain and a sudden 'black out' an adequate interpretation of such words as these?" the journalist asked rhetorically.

Continued on p. 19

Goldwynisms

The colossal movie mogul Samuel Goldwyn lived at the intersection of art and commerce. Though, to get there, he took a number of wrong linguistic turns. One of the great Hollywood pioneers, Goldwyn received producer credits on nearly 140 films, including such classics as *The Best Years of Our Lives, Guys and Dolls,* and *The Pride of the Yankees.* But when the movie mainstay died at age ninety-four in 1974, the *New York Times* conceded that "to the general public he was probably best known for his 'Goldwynisms,' the malapropisms, mixed metaphors, grammatical blunders and word manglings" that he was said to have uttered throughout his life.

Like baseball's Yogi Berra, Goldwyn didn't quite deserve all the credit he received for befuddling the English language. Late in his life Goldwyn would disavow connection to a number of them, and many in the business would back that claim. Admitted Charlie Chaplin in 1937 about some *Goldwynisms*: "It sounds like Sam Goldwyn. We'll pin it on Sam."

"Goldwynisms weren't the malapropisms that were always being attributed to him," three-time Oscar-nominated writer Garson Kanin said in 1974. "Most of them were invented by press agents."

As a result, when the *Oxford English Dictionary* included an entry on the producer's semantic contributions, they smartly hedged, describing a *Goldwynism* as a "witticism uttered by or typical of Samuel Goldwyn."

So, while Goldwyn may not have originated some (or many) of the following, know that when it comes to those that didn't come from his lips, he was the inspiration.

- "Anyone who goes to a psychiatrist should have his head examined."
- "A verbal contract isn't worth the paper it's written on."
- "Let's have some new clichés."
- "I'll give you a definite maybe."
- "I had a great idea this morning, but I didn't like it."
- "Let's bring it up-to-date with some snappy nineteenth-century dialogue."
- "We've got twenty-five years' worth of files out there, just sitting around. Now what I want you to do is to go out there and throw everything out—but make a copy of everything first."
- "The only trouble with this business is the dearth of bad pictures."
- "That's the trouble with directors—always biting the hand that lays the golden egg."
- "In two words: im possible."
- "I felt like we were on the brink of the abscess."
- "Our comedies are not to be laughed at."
- "I love the ground I walk on."
- "For this part I want a lady, somebody that's couth."
- "I want to make a picture about the Russian secret police: the GOP."
- "We've passed a lot of water since then."
- "I would be sticking my head in a moose."
- "Anything that man says you've got to take with a dose of salts."
- "Gentlemen, include me out."

Theater's sole domain over the word didn't last long. In the 1920s the expression was used to describe a temporary loss of vision. It occurred then (and now) to pilots who get hit by excessive g-force.

In the 1930s two additional *blackout* definitions emerged: loss of memory due to too much drinking and a loss of lights in your house due to a disruption in electricity.

Beyond those still-popular usages, the word reached newfound importance during World War II. In those years a *blackout* was essential as a way to prepare for Axis bombings. *Blackout* shades or turning off lights were required in England to prevent Nazi bombers above from being able to see any potential targets.

All that said, *blackout* has faded, so to speak, in theater circles.

Blockbuster
Patrick Huskinson designed the first *blockbuster* without the ability to watch a movie. The reason: Huskinson was blind.

If you're confused, here's another important fact: His work had nothing to do with box-office-winning films or the onetime ubiquitous video-rental chain of the same name. Instead, the British military man's contributions were even more impressive than the biggest Avengers *blockbuster*.

A distinguished pilot during World War I, Huskinson was playing a large role in armament production at the start of World War II when tragedy struck. A Nazi air bombing hit Huskinson's house, blinding him.

Undeterred, he continued to work and developed massive bombs, which were two tons or bigger and were so devastating that they were dubbed *blockbusters* for their capacity to destroy a whole city block. By 1942, articles lauding the bombs' value to the war effort were common in the United States.

For this contribution, Huskinson became a hero, receiving medals on both sides of the Atlantic. The English language also embraced his creation. Charles Lee, the literary editor of the *Philadelphia Record*, wrote a review of a 1944 book called *The Curtain Rises*, gushing that it was "destined to be a box-office blockbuster!"

Movie PR machines were regularly welcoming the term in the 1950s. But they weren't the only ones using it. The military still called big bombs *blockbusters* during that decade. The word also came up as part of the darker side of the fight for civil rights.

Blockbusting was used to describe introducing African-American families into white neighborhoods with the expectation that integration would send bigoted whites fleeing from the area. Real estate speculators would then follow up, purchasing properties from those leaving the community at below-value prices.

The 1968 Fair Housing Act aimed to outlaw this practice. Though it still persisted, this linguistic usage dwindled, leaving Hollywood with an open lane to appropriate the word. While it can be said that the film business took an already common expression, the industry's usage surely gave the term what any *blockbuster* at the theaters hopes for: longevity in the marketplace.

Bloopers

We may think of *bloopers* as harmless gaffes on TV or in everyday life, but in 1926 they were enough to cause a witch hunt in parts of the United States.

The term *blooper* emerged in the mid-1920s due to an early form of radio called a regenerative receiver. When the receiver was tuned poorly, not only would unwanted interference garble the owner's signal, but it would also distort or muddy his or her neighbors' radios as well.

In the early going the word *blooper* was used for "a person who has a regenerative receiving set and through ignorance does not know how to operate it, thereby making life a burden to his neighbors," explained a letter written into the Wisconsin Rapids (Wisconsin) *Daily Tribune* in 1924. That author further explained that these owners could "overcome this difficulty but it will take study and patience."

Despite those assurances, within two years, those living near these poorly handled radios in other towns across the country ran out of patience.

In Iowa the *Sumner Gazette* ran a front-page article in 1926, calling out a *blooper* who "has made the nights for a month past, hideous for other radio owners in town." It warned ominously that "the 'blooper' is courting sudden death" if the unidentified person didn't cut it out.

An ad that same year in the *Chester Times* (Pennsylvania) escalated the pursuit of *bloopers*. The notice ominously told readers that they could "help yourself and us to clear the air of Bloopers by filling in the coupon below with the name and address of any owner of a Blooper that is making trouble for you."

Thankfully, technology improved and nobody—that I can report—suffered sudden death from the awful interference. (Most believe that like *buzz* or *splat*, *blooper* was an onomatopoeia with *bloop* representing the sound the receivers made.)

The term likely led to a usage in baseball that began in the late 1930s. It refers to a softly hit fly ball that often lands for a base hit. But when it comes to its application for flubs of all sorts, a fellow by the name of Kermit Schafer deserves a lot of credit for its popularity.

Schafer started his career as a coordinator on live TV shows in New York. He almost lost his job one day when a refrigerator he was responsible for didn't open while on air. The mess-up gave him the idea to start putting together record albums and books with these sorts of embarrassing acts.

Blooper was already being used for blunders—particularly political ones—by the 1940s, but Schafer appropriated the word and became a huge success. His first record, "Pardon My Blooper," came out in 1952 and sold more than a million copies. By the time he died in 1979 at age sixty-four, he'd produced thirty-two records and fifteen books.

Though his work was sometimes controversial as he re-created some of the supposed *bloopers*, Schafer was always proud of his contribution to

Continued on p. 24

"Go ahead, make my day."
—"Dirty" Harry Callahan (Clint Eastwood), *Sudden Impact* (1983)

You know a film quote has made its way into the cultural bloodstream when the president of the United States uses it in a major policy speech less than sixteen months after the movie's release.

In March 1985 Ronald Reagan invoked Clint Eastwood's Dirty Harry character when speaking to business executives about his opposition to tax increases.

"No matter how well intentioned they might be, no matter what their illusions might be, I have my veto pen drawn and ready for any tax increase Congress might even think of sending up," he said. "And I have only one thing to say to the tax increasers: Go ahead, make my day."

The statement received laughs in the room and tons of media attention. Under the headline "Some New Material Is Needed," a *Washington Post* editorial panned its use.

Still, you can be sure that *Sudden Impact* screenwriter Joseph Stinson thought: mission accomplished.

Stinson, who had never written a feature screenplay before this film, was in a bit of a quandary. He knew that he would need to include a memorable moment as Eastwood's character was already known for the line "Do you feel lucky, punk?" from the 1971 film *Dirty Harry*. But at the same time, he recognized that it's nearly impossible to design a catchphrase to go viral.

"If you set yourself up to write that one-liner that's going to be iconic, you set yourself up to never have it happen," he said. "It's like Bruce Springsteen or Bob Dylan. They have those hits that people want to hear, but it's the last thing they want to play. You feel kind of cheated [if they don't play them], but then you hate it if it's not good enough."

Structurally speaking, there was precedent for this line, according to language expert Robert Hendrickson. The positive connotation of making someone's day dated back to the start of the twentieth century. In the 1909 novel *The Rosary*, a characters says, "I knew I wanted her; knew her presence made my day and her absence meant chill night. . . ."

But Stinson flipped the phrase to give it a smoldering anger. For the writer, who had worked in various areas of the industry, including acting, before getting this gig, it was all about coming up with a phrase that embodied the character's code of conduct.

"Once a method actor, always a method actor," he said. "I thought about the character. He lives by a code: 'This is what I am, this is what I'm going to do. You decide.'"

Despite the seemingly impossible task, Stinson knew he'd nailed it nearly immediately after coining the phrase.

"I'll be honest, I thought it was a pretty good line," he said. "I walked around L.A. testing it out in my imagination. If someone cut in front of me at midnight in the 'eight items or less' line, I'd give 'em the [Dirty Harry] squint." ★

American comedy. In a play on Alexander Pope's famed quote, he mused in his book *Prize Bloopers*: "To forgive is human, To err, divine."

Bogart

Stars—or their characters—have long lent their names to everyday items. The well-endowed actress Mae West inspired sailors to call bulky-in-the-chest life preservers *Mae Wests*. Then there are those short shorts called *Daisy Dukes*. The provocative pants are a nod to Catherine Bach's cut-off-jeans-wearing character of the same name in the 1980s series *The Dukes of Hazzard*.

But when it comes to this area of language, Humphrey Bogart may very well be in a category all his own. First off, rather than spawning a noun to describe an object, he was the motivating force for an action verb. (Sorry, Shirley Temple fans: Nobody ever says it's time to *Shirley Temple* when downing a soda.) Second, the idea of *bogarting* has led to not one but two different meanings.

In the 1960s *bogart* emerged as street slang for menacing or bullying another—or as *Ebony* magazine put it in 1965, to "muscle through." A generic example of usage: "The mean man better stop bogarting me." Most presume the star of such films as *Casablanca* and *The Maltese Falcon* received this honor because he so often played tough guys in the movies. As late as 1997 *Esquire* magazine was still using the term in this fashion.

Despite that definition, *bogarting* took on a totally different meaning in the late 1960s drug counterculture. In that world, *to bogart* meant to hog or act selfishly. Specifically, it was used when one person smoking a marijuana joint was slow to share it with others. Many sources say the reasoning behind this definition was that Bogart would often have a cigarette dangling from his mouth on the big screen as if he were jealously guarding it.

This version might have remained obscure if not for the 1968 song "Don't Bogart Me" by the Fraternity of Man. The tune, with its big line

"Don't Bogart that joint, my friend," was included in the iconic 1969 film *Easy Rider*, and this linguistic usage became well known.

Over the years, the greedy meaning has branched out beyond the dope-smoking world. For instance, in 1992 the *Washington Post*'s Tony Kornheiser (of future ESPN fame), mentioned *bogarting* in conjunction with doughnuts and an NBA player, while the film *Empire Records* (1995) featured a character talking about *bogarting* money. Nowadays, the term still exists—though more often than not, it's applied in some sort of parody of its original marijuana meaning.

Bombshell

The stunning actress Jean Harlow was known for her straight-talking comedic performances, but her legacy is mostly tied to the words used to describe her.

In 1931 the bright-flaxen-haired Harlow co-starred in the movie *Platinum Blonde*, which referenced the actress's look and popularized that term. Two years later she made an even bigger linguistic impact with the film *Bombshell*.

The term *bombshell* had already existed in a figurative sense since the nineteenth century to describe a destructive or shocking event or piece of news (e.g., "I can't believe John is moving to Kansas; what a *bombshell*!"). But Harlow's sex appeal gave the idiom, well, sex appeal. After the movie's release the word took on a new meaning for a devastatingly alluring woman. With advertising for the film often referring to the picture as *The Blonde Bombshell*, a subcategory—based on Harlow's golden hair color—also developed.

Harlow, who tragically died from kidney failure in 1937 at age twenty-six, remained in the public consciousness long after her passing, which surely helped maintain the expression's popularity. For example, in 1965—twenty-eight years after the actress's death—there was still enough interest in Harlow that two films and a book were produced about her life. (Admittedly, it helped that she had dramatic off-screen experiences that included three marriages, one of which ended in the mysterious suicide of her spouse just sixty-five days after their wedding.)

In 2001 a book called *The Bombshell Manual of Style* tried to break the concept down into its component parts. Among its tips to aspiring *bombshells*: Make sure you have the right name. "A Bombshell is never named Phyllis, Edith or Bertha," the book said. "And if she were you'd never know. Serious Bombshells take names with *va-va-voom*, breathy alliteration and starlet potential." Other advice included: "Every movement counts. A Bombshell never thoughtlessly enters a room or flops into a chair" and "The Bombshell respects tradition."

Lest you think this showbiz desire to box in stars based on appearance has only been confined to women, do note that *matinee idol looks* to describe a handsome actor (and ultimately as shortcut to reflect any good-looking man) predates *bombshell*. Devotees of the stage were calling dashing male thespians *matinee idols* before 1900.

Break a leg
Actors have been wishing colleagues the metaphorical catastrophe of a broken leg since the 1920s. It's a strange notion to say *break a leg* before going onstage (and nowadays by folks wishing the same before any big endeavor). Unfortunately, we're not quite sure how we got there. Still, we have a handful of potential origin stories.

We do know that in the eighteenth century, the phrase existed for a totally different purpose. If a woman had a child out of wedlock, she was said to have broken a leg. This usage seems like mere coincidence. Instead, here are some competing options straight from the theater:

It started with the imagery of bowing (see *Take a bow*, p. 175). When a woman bows to accept praise after a performance, she bends— or as we could alternatively say, breaks—her legs. So, in other words, wishing someone the opportunity to bow numerous times (and figuratively breaking legs over and over again) would be a good thing. The only problem is men didn't necessarily bow with the same leg action so this doesn't seem to cover all performers.

An alternative is that it has to do with the Elizabethan British practice of throwing coins at thespians after a good performance. To pick up the loose change, you need to bend down and, so to speak, break your leg.

The sixteenth century had the phrase *make a leg* to reflect bowing, and breaking the same bit of anatomy might just be a linguistic twist on the older expression.

It could also fall under the avoid-the-jinx category. French actors say *merde* (an expletive for feces) before going onstage as a way to sidestep tempting the gods to unleash calamity. If you were to say "good luck," the theory goes, you'd undoubtedly get the opposite. *Break a leg* falls into this category.

Then there's the assertion that it's a linguistic misinterpretation. Jewish actors would sometimes say *hatslakha u'braka*, which means "success and blessing," to one another before beginning a performance. (Apparently, they weren't afraid of the whole jinx thing.) Supposedly non-Jewish actors misunderstood and changed it to *break a leg*. Similarly, there's a claim that the German phrase *Hals und Beinbruch* ("break a neck and a leg"), which was used by World War I German pilots as a wry wink at saying "good luck," could have been the starting point.

Finally, there are a few possibilities that are a bit more outlandish. One is that people were suggesting to emulate the great stage actress Sarah Bernhardt, who continued to work even after having a leg amputated late in her career. Clearly, suffering a broken leg would have only a tenuous tie to Bernhardt's situation. Others even suggest that Abraham Lincoln assassin John Wilkes Booth is somehow involved. He broke a leg jumping from the theater balcony after shooting the president. Inexplicably, some think that inspired people.

"Here's looking at you, kid."
—Rick Blaine (Humphrey Bogart),
Casablanca (1942)

Casablanca, which was loosely based on a play called *Everybody Comes to Rick's*, had seven writers work on its script. Twin brothers Jules and Philip Epstein, who came up with the classic line "round up the usual suspects," and Howard Koch received credit (and an Oscar) for their efforts. But others like Casey Robinson (*Captain Blood*), who worked on the romantic flashbacks, also contributed.

Another person who might deserve some writing recognition: Humphrey Bogart.

According to *Casablanca* expert Aljean Harmetz, there's legitimate reason to believe that he ad-libbed the oft-quoted statement "Here's looking at you, kid." What's particularly surprising is that he may have very well been inspired by a series of poker games.

The ironclad facts are that the first time Bogart uses the words in the movie (he'd end up uttering them three times in the film), the dialogue was not in the mimeographed script. Instead, it was added in pencil. As a result, we know the dialogue was inserted that day.

Beyond that, we need to take the word of the on-set PR person. According to the unit publicist's notes, Ingrid Bergman's hairdresser and English coach would teach the actress how to play poker during set breaks. Every once in a while, Bogart would look in. Since the Swedish Bergman, who played the female lead Ilsa Lund, didn't know English slang, the actor taught her "Here's looking at you" during one session to use as part of her card-playing banter. This supposedly inspired the line.

While others have theorized that the Epstein brothers conjured the expression, and it's hard to argue this anecdote doesn't have a far-fetched quality to it, Harmetz concluded, "the incident seems too odd to have been invented."

If it did happen this way, Bogart wasn't the only unexpected resource for the movie's great dialogue. One of the big problems when shooting commenced was that nobody knew how to end the film. Would Bogart's Rick get Bergman's Ilsa, or would she board the plane with Victor Laszlo (Paul Henreid)? It's common lore that Bergman kept asking director Michael Curtiz whom she'd end up with because the actress wanted to know how to subtly indicate her feelings in earlier scenes.

In the end the *Casablanca* brain trust decided (spoiler alert!) to leave Rick with Captain Louis Renault (Claude Rains) and without the girl. Yet, even after that was resolved and the movie completed principal photography, the film's producer, Hal Wallis, wasn't satisfied. He called for reshoots and ordered the use of one of two lines to close the film—either "Luis [sic], I might have known you'd mix your patriotism with a little larceny" or "Luis [sic], I think this is the beginning of a beautiful friendship."

Movie fans everywhere can rejoice to this day that the filmmakers chose the latter. Final point: One phrase that never came from anybody involved with the film was "Play it again, Sam." The actual statement from Bergman's character was "Play it, Sam. Play 'As Time Goes By.'" ★

Bringing down the house

You don't need to be an actor to want to *bring down the house*. Politicians have long relied on a bit of manipulative speechifying to do the trick. For more than a century and a half, one surefire way to accomplish this task has been to harken back to the country's early settlers.

"It is the fashion for public speakers . . . [to] introduc[e] some allusion to our revolutionary pilgrim ancestry, as it is sure, in theatrical parlance, to 'bring down the house'—in other words, to produce two or three rounds of hearty applause," a publication called *Flag of Our Union* explained in 1854.

When that newspaper invoked this metaphor for creating such excitement that the rafters would figuratively descend, it had been around in the stage world for at least one hundred years. Calling a theater a *house* is even older. Writers in Old English first used that word as shorthand for *playhouse* sometime before the 1500s. (*Geek note*: From there we also got the expression *full house* by the seventeenth century to describe a packed theater; for poker players, calling a hand a *full house* didn't come along until the 1800s, long after the theatrical business began using it.)

Despite the great desire by performers both inside and outside of show business to *bring down the house*, it evidently isn't something you want to do in every venue—full or otherwise. In 1879 a writer for the *New York Evangelist* laid in to religious figures who pandered to their audiences in this way: "It is a shameful thing for the preacher to 'bring down the house,' to induce laughter and applause by funny or grotesque sayings," the correspondent warned.

While there are no documented cases of great applause or laughter literally bringing down an establishment, there have been instances when theaters have shaken to the point that patrons thought it was coming down. According to etymologist Robert Hendrickson, during a seventeenth-century British performance of Christopher Marlowe's classic play *Dr. Faustus*, which tells the story of a man willing to trade his soul with the devil, the timbers at a London playhouse began to crack, and fear of the building collapsing gripped the audience.

Some wondered whether the shaky structural integrity was caused by the fiendish topic of the production rather than sterling performances. But in the end the theater held up—though other than ruling out the excitement of the crowd, nobody ever discovered what led to the house almost coming down.

Cast of thousands

Before the days of computer-generated imagery, nothing said *epic* in filmmaking like a *cast of thousands*. At the dawn of the blockbuster, director D. W. Griffith used thousands of extras for Civil War battle scenes to great effect in his controversial 1915 opus *The Birth of a Nation*. Though he would wisecrack that he could only afford their pay because he'd "worked out an infallible system. Our soldiers use real bullets."

Even when shortcuts were required, these hordes of humanity still delivered. For instance, in *Gone with the Wind* producer David O. Selznick orchestrated a wide shot showing a mass of wounded Confederate soldiers. The plan was to employ about a thousand background actors, but it didn't look right so he dressed up 680 dummies to go along with live extras to get the desired result. No matter, when *Gone with the Wind* author Margaret Mitchell went to the film's Atlanta premiere, she was impressed. "My god," she reportedly whispered to Clark Gable while the scene was playing, "if we'd had as many soldiers as that, we'd have won the war."

As you'd expect, these scenes were not easy to choreograph. One story to this end involves director William Wellman. During the filming of *Wings*, which would go on to win the first-ever best picture Oscar, Wellman decided to reenact a World War I battle complete

Continued on p. 34

> ## "Houston, we have a problem."
> ## —Jim Lovell (Tom Hanks),
> ## *Apollo 13* (1995)

In Hollywood the truth—no matter how inherently jaw-dropping—can always be tweaked a bit for additional effect. Such was the case with *Apollo 13*. By all accounts director Ron Howard wanted to emphasize authenticity with the movie. After all, how much do you really need to change to create tension when the real-life story centers on astronauts potentially getting marooned in space more than two hundred thousand miles from earth?

And yet, there was a way. In 1970, when this potential tragedy actually happened, astronaut Jack Swigert first alerted to mission control by saying, "Okay, Houston, I believe we've had a problem here." When mission control asked for clarification, the crew's commander, Jim Lovell, quickly followed up by reiterating "Houston, we've had a problem."

In the movie, Swigert, who was played by Kevin Bacon, doesn't deliver the fateful words, and Tom Hanks's Lovell instead offers "Houston, we have a problem."

A decade after the film was released, Hanks seemed disappointed by the modification.

"You know . . . it's actually a mistake on my part, because I believe Jim actually said, 'Houston, we've had a problem,'" the actor said on the *Today* show in 2005. "It was in the script, and I never bothered to think that, 'Well, let's go back and make sure that's the correct tense.'"

In defense of screenwriters William Broyles Jr. and Al Reinert, who were nominated for a best adapted screenplay Oscar, the change to present tense added to the tension and, without it, this line probably wouldn't have earned its status in popular culture. The slight modification was one that didn't go unnoticed by *New York Times* critic Janet Maslin when the film was released.

"The line of dialogue that will be best remembered from Ron Howard's absolutely thrilling new 'Apollo 13' is a slight variation on the truth," Maslin wrote in 1995. "It's a small but important change, one more way that 'Apollo 13' unfolds with perfect immediacy, drawing viewers into the nail-biting suspense of a spellbinding true story." ★

with a couple of thousand extras and tons of pyrotechnics. To start the scene, the filmmaker made sure everyone knew that he planned on waving a red flag to commence the mayhem. Standing on a tower with some observers, he was about ready to go when the battle began prematurely. Startled, he looked around for an explanation and saw one of his guests, a little girl. She had picked up the flag and was using it to wave to a friend.

As a turn of phrase, *cast of thousands* emerged at the same time as these first extravaganzas. In January 1916 the *Laredo Times* (Texas) gushed that the local theater would be running *Cabiria*, which cost "the immense sum of $300,000 to produce" and featured "a cast of thousands of people."

Like the filmgoers who enjoyed these spectacles, writers were drawn to the expression as a metaphor for any large group. In the run-up to the 1928 presidential election, the *New York Times* said the Democratic Party was lining up supporters to stump for candidates, or, as the newspaper put it, "a cast of thousands of actors . . . will speak their parts from political platforms in every State."

Catcall

We all know that it isn't socially acceptable to whistle at a lady walking down the street. And yet, resorting to a *catcall* was once a respectable (and handy) activity commonly used at theaters.

Back in the seventeenth century, a *catcall* was the name of a small whistle-like instrument that could fit in a pocket. Rather than replicating birdsong, the little apparatus let off a noise that sounded like a squealing animal when blown. Its purpose? To give patrons of the stage an easy way to express disgust or impatience with a performance.

In 1712 a prominent writer and politician named Joseph Addison penned a widely read tongue-in-cheek essay for his popular magazine the *Spectator* about the role the *catcall* played in theaters. After joking that he had difficulty buying one because London's actors had purchased them all up in a preemptory bid to avoid ridicule, Addison mockingly discussed how an instrument of such simplicity—and harm to performers' egos—must be ancient. (Ultimately, though, he concluded that nobody used it better than British audiences, wryly observing, "The cat-call exerts itself to most advantage in the British theatre: it very much improves the sound of nonsense. . . .")

On a (slightly) more serious note, Addison did remark that it was a sound that could be intimidating for any player. "The cat-call," he wrote, "has struck a damp into generals, and frightened heroes off the stage. At the first sound of it I have seen a crowned head tremble and a princess fall into fits."

Addison's article, which was reprinted in compilations of his work for more than a century after it was originally written, surely kept the word in the public consciousness. But how it made the transition onto the street for construction workers to use isn't wholly clear.

By the mid-1700s the term *catcall* was being applied not only for the instrument but also for instances when people would try to replicate the sound under any circumstance without the device. This put the term in the linguistic bloodstream outside of the theater. It took a while, but over the years *catcalls* traveled well. We know this because the *Oxford English Dictionary* indicates that defining a *catcall* as "a whistle, cry or suggestive comment intended to express sexual attraction or attractiveness" was developed far from the streets of London—it was created in the United States during the twentieth century.

However, the long length of time it took for the word to transition into a term for a lascivious maneuver shouldn't be surprising. After all, in 1839 a natural history magazine was still describing the sound in a way that would never be confused with sexiness. The article explained that "the horrible wailings of pain or fighting . . . give[s] name to the noisy and discordant instrument of disapprobation, the catcall."

Whatchoo talkin' 'bout? Memorable Prime-Time TV Lines

Over the past decade the debate has raged: Which is better, film or television? The medium of television has boasted so many series in recent years that we'll watch again and again (think: *Breaking Bad, Mad Men, Downton Abbey, House of Cards,* do I need to go on?), while movies have experienced their fair share of forgettable pictures (if you haven't erased *Paul Blart: Mall Cop 2* from your brain, you should).

We can argue over quality, but one thing is certain: From a language perspective, when we talk historically about memorable dialogue, films have tended to be a bit stickier in our minds than television. You didn't need to live through the 1930s to know *The Wizard of Oz*'s "*There's no place like home*" (see p. 140). On the contrary, with a few notable exceptions, TV quotes have typically been most unforgettable for those who experienced them in their own time. For instance, while baby boomers can easily recall "*Sock it to me*," the statement will leave the vast majority of millennials stumped. Do you disagree? Decide for yourself. Below is a chronological list of some of the most iconic prime-time TV quotes and catchphrases. That said, even if some of these jog just a faint memory, with the ever-increasing quality of TV, perhaps, the tide will change in generations to come.

- "Lucy, you got some 'splaining to do!"—*I Love Lucy* (1951-1957)
- "Good night, and good luck"—*See It Now* (1951-1958)
- "Baby, you're the greatest," "Pow! Right in the kisser," "How sweet it is," and "Bang, zoom! Straight to the moon!"—*The Honeymooners* (1955-1956)

- "Next stop: The Twilight Zone"—*The Twilight Zone* (1959-1964)
- "Yabba dabba do!"—*The Flintstones* (1960-1966)
- "Danger, Will Robinson"—*Lost in Space* (1965-1968)
- "You rang?"—*The Addams Family* (1964-1966)
- "Would you believe . . ."—*Get Smart* (1965-1970)
- "Live long and prosper" and "Space, the final frontier"—*Star Trek* (1966-1969)
- "This tape will self-destruct in five seconds"—*Mission: Impossible* (1966-1973)
- "Mom always liked you best"—*The Smothers Brothers Comedy Hour* (1967-1970)
- "Sock it to me"—*Rowan & Martin's Laugh-In* (1967-1973)
- "Book 'em, Danno"—*Hawaii Five-O* (1968-1980)
- "Marcia, Marcia, Marcia!"—*The Brady Bunch* (1969-1974)
- "And now for something completely different"—*Monty Python's Flying Circus* (1969-1974)
- "What you see is what you get!"—*The Flip Wilson Show* (1970-1974)
- "Just one more thing . . ."—*Columbo* (1971-1978)
- "Stifle!"—*All in the Family* (1971-1979)
- "Good night, John Boy"—*The Waltons* (1971-1981)
- "Who loves you, baby?"—*Kojak* (1973-1978)
- "Dyn-o-mite"—*Good Times* (1974-1979)
- "Sit on it" and "Aaay!"—*Happy Days* (1974-1984)
- "Up your nose with a rubber hose"—*Welcome Back, Kotter* (1975-1979)
- "Kiss my grits!"—*Alice* (1976-1985)
- "De plane! De plane!"—*Fantasy Island* (1977-1984)
- "Nanu-nanu"—*Mork & Mindy* (1978-1982)
- "Tenk you veddy much"—*Taxi* (1978-1983)

- "Whatchoo talkin' 'bout, Willis?"—*Diff'rent Strokes* (1978-1986)
- "Let's be careful out there"—*Hill Street Blues* (1981-1987)
- "Norm!"—*Cheers* (1982-1993)
- "I love it when a plan comes together"—*The A-Team* (1983-1987)
- "Yada, yada, yada," "No soup for you!," "Newman . . .," and "Not that there's anything wrong with that"—*Seinfeld* (1989-1998)
- "Did I do that?"—*Family Matters* (1989-1998)
- "D'oh!," "Ay caramba," "Don't have a cow, man," and "Eat my shorts"—*The Simpsons* (1989-)
- "Homey don't play that"—*In Living Color* (1990-1994)
- "The truth is out there"—*The X-Files* (1993-2002, 2016)
- "How *you* doin'?"—*Friends* (1994-2004)
- "Holy crap!"—*Everybody Loves Raymond* (1996-2005)
- "Here is your moment of Zen"—*The Daily Show* (1996-)
- "Oh, my God! They killed Kenny!"—*South Park* (1997-)
- "Is that your final answer?"—*Who Wants to Be a Millionaire?* (1998-)
- "The tribe has spoken"—*Survivor* (2000-)
- "You are the weakest link. Goodbye"—*Weakest Link* (2001-2002 in the US; 2000-2012 in the UK)
- "Tell me what you don't like about yourself"—*Nip/Tuck* (2003-2010)
- "I've made a huge mistake"—*Arrested Development* (2003-)
- "Who's your daddy?"—*Veronica Mars* (2004-2007)
- "Guys . . . where are we?"—*Lost* (2004-2010)
- "Everybody lies"—*House* (2004-2012)
- "You're fired!"—*The Apprentice* (2004-)
- "That's what *she* said"—*The Office* (2005-2013)
- "It's gonna be *legen* . . . wait for it . . . *dary*"—*How I Met Your Mother* (2005-2014)

- "Clear eyes, full hearts, can't lose"—*Friday Night Lights* (2006-2011)
- "Blerg" and "I want to go to there"—*30 Rock* (2006-2013)
- "Bazinga"—*The Big Bang Theory* (2007-)

Cattle call

While some in the movie industry might be convinced that their business created the idea of treating individuals like livestock, contemptuously calling people *cattle* is a centuries-old allusion. Writers in the 1500s used it in this fashion (and William Shakespeare utilized it in *As You Like It* at the beginning of the 1600s).

Nevertheless, Hollywood's unique contribution to this metaphor is the *cattle call*. The most popular story about the expression is that it started with Alfred Hitchcock. The legendary director was well known for being tough on actors and supposedly said, "Actors are cattle." This claim was so ceaseless that a journalist once asked Hitchcock if he made the statement. Various sources quote him differently, but Hitchcock supposedly said something to the effect of: "I have been misquoted. What I really said is: Actors should be treated as cattle."

Whatever Hitchcock's involvement, *cattle call* was in the Hollywood lexicon by 1952. But how did we get from *cattle* to *cattle call*?

One potential explanation is a song called "Cattle Call," which was popular at the time. Written in 1934 by Tex Owens, this tune was once named the sixteenth-greatest Western song of all time by the Western Writers of America. It was recorded by Eddy Arnold in 1944 and became his signature song, eventually hitting the top spot on the country music charts. In view of the timing, it's quite possible that whoever applied this phrase figuratively had this song rattling in his or her brain.

Even with that notoriety, show business's definition for the phrase was still working its way beyond Hollywood and New York in the

1960s. In 1961 a stunned writer for the *San Antonio Light* penned an article about how scores of beautiful women were being shuttled in for a modelling audition in New York (for *audition*, see p. 2). After riding down an elevator with a couple of failed candidates who called the event "Just another 'cattle call,'" the journalist admitted, "I had never heard the phrase before. Nor had I ever heard a more accurate one."

Nowadays, the expression has branched out to mean any sort of mass of humanity being herded. For instance, the *Wall Street Journal* applied it to air travel in 2008. "The airline used to board passengers in three main groups—a cattle-call system that irritated many road warriors," the paper said.

Cleavage

For nearly twenty years Joe Breen was one of the most powerful men in Hollywood. From 1934 to 1954 (with the exception of a brief hiatus in 1941–42), he was the movie industry's chief censor. Though he'd describe himself as "too fat and too genial" to be thought of as a prude, he would edit some 3,000 scripts a year for morals and good taste.

Among the many issues he tackled were breasts. While tight sweaters could sometimes be okay, showing a bit too much skin was a big no-no. This region of a woman's chest had been known as *décolletage* (from a fashion term for a low-cut top) since at least the late 1800s, but Breen and his team opted for a new euphemism and chose *cleavage*.

Historically speaking, the term was an odd choice. In the early nineteenth century, it was primarily a piece of geological jargon for separating (or *cleaving*) rocks and crystals. By the end of that century, it had taken on metaphorical meaning for groups or opinions that were being split apart. In the 1930s newspapers were commonly using it in reference to political fissions. An example: "The Mason and Dixon line has for many years been, and will for years to come be, the line of political cleavage," an Amarillo, Texas, paper wrote in 1930.

Maybe Breen and his colleagues saw an offbeat connection in taking what had become a term reflecting divisiveness and applying it to sex—something that can be very political in and of itself. But if that were the case, there wasn't too much humor in the code's definition for the word. According to *Time* magazine, Breen's very academic sounding *cleavage* was "the shadowed depression dividing an actress's bosom into two distinct sections."

This internal use of *cleavage* was outed in 1946 because of a British film called *The Wicked Lady*. In England the movie was a big hit and even received a royal stamp of approval. At the 1945 premier of the film, Queen Mary called it "rather nice," according to the *Times* of London. But Breen found the low-cut dresses inappropriate for American audiences and called for changes in the film in order to get his organization's seal of approval, which was effectively necessary to distribute the picture in the United States.

The *cleavage* (in the opinion sense) between Breen and the film's producers was widely reported by the national media, with everybody from the *New York Times* to *Life* magazine making reference to this new use of the word. The movie was eventually altered, but the term's carnal meaning was embraced so quickly that even a 1948 article in the Canadian hamlet of Medicine Hat referred to Rita Hayworth's "cleavage" without having to explain what they were talking about.

Cliffhanger
Hollywood was built on the old adage "always leave them wanting more," and no plot device embodies that more than the *cliffhanger*. The concept, which was developed in the early days of movie serials, goes like this: At the height of a riveting dramatic sequence, rather than offer resolution, save the moment for the next installment. Modern TV execs love this. Think, "Who Shot J.R.?" on *Dallas* or the final episode for just about any season of *Game of Thrones*. As for the early days, this

Continued on p. 44

> **"I coulda been a contender."**
> **—Terry Malloy (Marlon Brando),**
> *On the Waterfront* **(1954)**

Boxer Roger Donoghue knew a lot about what it took to be a contender. When the twenty-year-old entered the ring at Madison Square Garden on April 29, 1951, he was a middleweight sporting an impressive 25-2-1 record and a winner's nickname: the Golden Boy. But that night he hit his opponent, George Flores, so hard with a combination of punches in the eighth round that he not only knocked the fighter out but also ultimately killed him.

Following the tragedy, Donoghue's championship dreams left him. He half-heartedly boxed three more times but lost twice and retired. To his credit, he gave his purse for one of those final fights to the grieving Flores family.

While the story is objectively sad, Donoghue entered his post-fight life with a great attitude and became friends with many of New York's elite, including writers like Norman Mailer and Budd Schulberg, who would win an Oscar for penning the screenplay to *On the Waterfront*.

In passing one day, Schulberg asked Donoghue about what could have been in his career if not for the forlorn Flores fight.

Donoghue said, "Well, I was pretty good, but I have that Irish skin and I cut pretty easily. I guess I could have been a contender," Schulberg recounted in 2006. "He didn't make a big deal of it, but it really stuck in my mind."

Schulberg was very involved with the fight game, and along with writing on it, he actually ran a gym and managed a heavyweight wannabe contender named Archie McBride who once fought the great Floyd Patterson. Familiar with the pathos of the ring, Schulberg discarded Donoghue's matter-of-fact attitude but kept the words and gave them to Marlon Brando's melancholy character Terry Malloy.

The statement resonated so greatly because so many people—regardless of station in life—could relate to it. In 2010 *Psychology Today* ran an article about feeling like you're falling short, calling that emotion the "Contender Syndrome" in honor of the film line.

"Whether it's a 16-year-old student or 45-year-old CFO, I hear them say, 'I'm not as successful as I should be,' and I'm seeing it more and more," San Francisco psychologist Jim Taylor said in the article. "It used to be that your immediate comparison group was your neighborhood or friends. Now you're exposed to everybody who has so much. We base our happiness on our most immediate comparison group. These days, it's the world."

The piece offered a handful of ways to avoid ending up like Malloy (well, at least when it comes to feeling bad about yourself; you're on your own when it comes to sidestepping gangsters). The writer Abby Ellin suggested the following strategies: working smart rather than hard; preparing backup plans; reminding yourself of your achievements; and noting that you likely have success that others only dream of attaining. ★

form of nail-biting nonending could include everything from leaving a lady tied on train tracks as the black-hatted villain twirled his handlebar mustache to having a hero hanging for dear life from an actual cliff.

Some believe that literal cliffhanger was innovated by the British author Thomas Hardy, who between September 1872 and July 1873 serialized his novel *A Pair of Blue Eyes* in London's *Tinsley's Magazine*. In it, the hero Knight can be found clinging to a cliff asking the fateful question, "Was Death really stretching out his hand?"

Hardy certainly made his mark on the movies, inspiring films with such books as *Jude the Obscure* and *Tess of the d'Urbervilles*, but even if his cliffhanger led to some copycat moviemaking, it's unlikely his original plot point directly spawned the term. While this genre of movies emerged around 1914 (a serial called *The Perils of Pauline* is often credited as the first great production in this style), it doesn't appear that the term reached general publication print until the start of the 1930s, suggesting the derivative use of *cliffhangers* deserves more credit than Hardy for ultimately giving us the 1993 Sylvester Stallone actioner *Cliffhanger*.

Still, it's probable that the expression predated its known written use because when it finally showed up in publications, readers were clearly expected to know what it was. For example, a 1931 issue of the Hollywood trade newspaper *Variety* reported some bad news for a "cliff hanger" serial from Universal Pictures called *Battling Buffalo Bill*. The article, which was an early reference in that publication to this style of moviemaking, gave no explanation of the term. (Fun fact: The problem with the project was a fresh-faced twenty-four-year-old actor named John Wayne was all set to star, but Columbia Pictures, which had him under contract, wouldn't allow him to studio-jump and work on the project.)

Nowadays, cliffhangers aren't limited to action on the screen. During the 2013 sequestration battle in Congress, PBS put together an online guide to explain the situation as people waited nervously to see whether a deal could be struck. The title for the compendium: "'Cliffhanger' Interactive: A Guide to the Gridlock."

Cloak-and-dagger

When it comes to the espionage and subterfuge that the expression *cloak-and-dagger* represents, the great Spanish playwright Lope de Vega undoubtedly had a deep personal understanding of the phrase's meaning.

Born in 1562, Lope, whose work served as a starting point for the expression, was a prolific writer who some have claimed penned up to 1,800 plays. But beyond his inexhaustible output for the stage, he lived a dramatic life. He served in the Spanish Armada for a time and was a major operator at the court of Madrid. He also had tempestuous love affairs, including one with a married woman, which led to a stint in prison and exile to Castile for eight years.

All of this must have been great fodder for his plays *de capa y espada* (translation: of cloak and sword). Though this style existed when Lope went to work, his ability to create intrigue in these productions, which gained their name from the fact that the upper-middle-class characters typically wore large capes and swords, brought wide attention to the genre. Featuring questions of honor, duels, jealousy, and a whole lot of misunderstandings, this form of theater became so widely popular that it eventually spread to France, where it was called *de cape et d'épée* (again, of cloak and sword).

But when the melodramas came to Britain, they got a title change to *cloak-and-dagger*. The connection seems clear, but some have nevertheless wondered whether *cloak-and-dagger* shows gave us the expression that became so popular for talking about real-world plotting and conspiracy during the twentieth century (remember: Cold War).

In 1769 a letter printed in a British periodical called the *Gentleman's Magazine* offered a metaphorically similar statement that had nothing to do with the stage. In it, a discussion about the potential result of simmering tensions between the American colonies and Great Britain includes the statement: "Those who endeavor to dissolve it, carry a dagger under the cloak of patriotism to stab their country to the heart."

Continued on p. 48

> ## "I love the smell of napalm in the morning."
> ## —Lieutenant Colonel Kilgore (Robert Duvall),
> ## *Apocalypse Now* (1979)

When screenwriter John Milius wrote this line, he had his doubts about its viability.

"That scene with Robert Duvall on the beach, I thought, 'That's so over the top; that's going to end up on the cutting room [floor]," Milius said in 2008.

If the *Apocalypse Now* brain trust had gone with its original plan for the movie, he may have very well been right. The idea for this film began while Milius was at film school at the University of Southern California. A professor believed that a successful film adaptation of *Heart of Darkness* was impossible. Milius, who said that claim was "like waving a red flag in front of a bull," took on the challenge.

While still in college, Milius would talk to classmate George Lucas about the idea, and when they finished school, they agreed that Lucas would direct the movie. Lucas's take on the project was to do a small film in a documentary style. Milius even discussed going to Vietnam to shoot some real-life footage. (*Geek note:* The film's name was a play on a popular hippie button that featured a peace sign and said "Nirvana Now"; to counter the counterculture, Milius modified it so that the peace sign looked like a bomber and replaced "Nirvana" with "Apocalypse.")

Everything appeared set until Lucas found success with *American Graffiti*. With his new clout, Lucas now had the ability to do another long-simmering idea, *Star Wars*. So Francis Ford Coppola stepped in. Unlike Lucas, Coppola liked the idea of an epic incendiary picture. Helicopters flying in attack mode to the music of Richard Wagner's *Ride of the Valkyries*, and Lieutenant Colonel Bill Kilgore's intense attack plans aligned well with Milius's intentions.

This scene was in the writer's original screenplay draft. The only major difference: Milius, who would be nominated alongside Coppola for best adapted screenplay for this work, had originally named the surf-loving commander Colonel Kharnage. That name was ultimately discarded as too obvious. Instead, they went with the similarly meaning, but modestly more subtle, Kilgore. ★

Still, the first known written example of the exact expression was by Charles Dickens in his 1841 book *Barnaby Rudge*. In that instance, the great writer satirically mentioned *cloak-and-dagger* in reference to the form of plays that had been made renowned by Lope some two centuries earlier, making the link unmistakable.

A final point: *Cloak-and-dagger* isn't the only stage genre that's earned broader use in the English language. *Sturm und Drang*, which is German for "storm and stress," was the title of a 1776 play by Friedrich Maximilian Klinger. The production inspired a style of intensely emotional theater and has since been taken to describe any sort of powerful real-world drama. The broad range of people who have used that phrase have ranged from talk-show host Geraldo Rivera to historian Doris Kearns Goodwin (also see *melodramatic*, p. 109).

Close-up

The *close-up* was heresy in the early days of film.

Pioneering director D. W. Griffith is generally credited with bringing this shooting style to Hollywood. But the first time he showed footage of these snugly framed images to his financiers, they supposedly flipped.

"We paid for the whole actor, Mr. Griffith; we want to see all of him," Henry Marvin, who was the head of Biograph, where Griffith was working, was said to have exclaimed.

As the story goes, Griffith, who began making movies in 1908, was quick to defend his artistic decision.

"Museums are full of masterpieces with nothing but large and arresting faces," he said. "If the face tells what I mean it to tell, an audience will forget about the legs, arms, liver, and lungs."

Griffith wasn't the only early filmmaker to get grief over opting for close-ups.

When French director Abel Gance used them in his 1917 film *Barberousse*, he received a similar reaction to Griffith's lambasting.

"What are these huge pictures supposed to mean?" the film's producer, Louis Nalpas, asked. "You'll have people panicking in the cinema. They'll make for the exits!"

Of course, the anxiety was misplaced. Griffith employed close-ups in his groundbreaking *The Birth of a Nation*. Though the movie's stance on race was morally dubious, it was declared one of Hollywood's first blockbusters.

In his 1913 book *Technique of the Photoplay*, Epes Winthrop "E. W." Sargent provided one of the first technical discussions on the term—though Sargent actually applied a different word for a tight close-up, calling it a "bust" shot.

"Properly speaking," he wrote, "a bust is a portrait showing the head and shoulders only, but bust is more definite than *close-up*, which is sometimes used, for close-up might also mean a full picture, but with the camera closer to the scene."

Before long the *close-up* was widely applied for tight face shots and, by the 1920s, for any sort of intimate or detailed examination (as in "this book provides a *close-up* on Hollywood idioms").

Still, one question remains: Are close-ups worn-out in most movies? Tony Bill, who won an Oscar for producing *The Sting* and has directed a number of other films, offered the following advice for would-be filmmakers: "Collect as many as possible while shooting, but in the editing room, use with caution: It's easy to overdose."

Cue

Like *ad-lib* (see p. 1), *cue* made its debut as an abbreviation. In the sixteenth century, *playbooks* would often include the simple notation *q*. This was short for the Latin word *quando*, which means "when." In other words, if an actor saw a *q* in his script, it told him it was time to speak his lines. Phonetically, *cue* is how the stage direction was uttered aloud and, ultimately, became how it was written. The oldest known reference dates to 1553 and by the 1600s it was generally being used as a hint or a direction to act or proceed in a certain way.

Since, *cue* has become the centerpiece for such idioms as *take your cue* (for taking directions), *that's my cue* (for it's my turn), and *as if on cue* (for something happening at the perfect time). The word has also proved important in the TV and radio worlds. A *cue light* is the name for the special light that goes on when a radio or TV show is on the air or recording. *Cue cards* are those pieces of cardboard that provide scripted lines for on-camera performers.

What's less certain is whether the theatrical use of *cue* led to the always popular *miscue* to describe a mistake or error. Some dictionaries have claimed it comes from the stage, where it's shorthand for "a slip of the tongue." But *miscue* also became a popular term in billiards in the middle of the 1800s. While the theater definition suggests a little mistake, a pool *miscue*, as in mishitting a ball with a cue stick, indicates a slightly more serious mess-up. The billiards meaning seems to line up a little better with our common usage of the word for a gaffe. In addition, the figurative use of *miscue* saw a sharp rise in the final decades of the 1800s (right when it was showing up regularly in newspapers in conjunction with reports on billiard matches). This makes pool halls the likely source for popularizing this connotation.

Whether or not the theater gave us *miscue*, you can be sure of one thing: A *queue*, as in a line of people, comes from a completely different place. It may be pronounced the same a *cue*, but *queue* is a French word that means *tail* and is originally derived from a different Latin word, *coda*.

Curtains (the curtain falls)

Over the centuries, the fall of the theater curtain has been a popular metaphor for life. Everyone should be able to relate to the poignant words South African author Olive Schreiner penned in 1883 about our fragile mortal condition: "When the curtain falls, no one is ready."

A variety of analogies featuring the final curtain closing date back to at least the seventeenth century. Americans were using it during colonial days. "Ah! The tale is told—the scene is ended—and the curtain falls" were the first words of a 1775 obituary in the *Pennsylvania Magazine*.

While saying the *curtain falls*, *the curtain has drawn*, or *the curtain closes* have long histories (interestingly, saying the *curtain opens* for the start of life hasn't been quite as pervasive), another construction, *it's curtains*, is relatively new.

To be sure, the expression seems like a Damon Runyon–esque line put in the mouths of mobsters in the 1920s. Just go to YouTube to see a wise-guy-talking Bugs Bunny lampooning that usage in a 1946 cartoon with the famous tough guy actor Edgar G. Robinson. The rabbit menaces Robinson's animated character Rocky, saying, "It's curtains for ya . . ." before putting a set of drapes on the gangster's head.

In truth, the metaphorical expression is actually a little older, showing up in the first decade of the 1900s. When boxing great Bob Fitzsimmons lost a big fight to Bill Lang in 1909, an article in the *Fort Wayne Sentinel* (Indiana) opened with this succinct conclusion about the aging fighter's career: "It's curtains for Bob Fitzsimmons."

For those who are literal-minded, theater curtains come in a variety of designs—all of which have colorful names of their own. The main curtain has been known as the front curtain, grand drape, main drape, or main rag. Versions include the Austrian, the waterfall, the brail, the traveler, the Venetian, and the wipe.

The traveler, which is also sometimes known as a bi-parting curtain or draw curtain, is the most common and, generally, the least expensive. Often made of velvet, it's the basic kind that's made of two pieces and parts vertically in the middle.

For those looking for class, the Austrian, which looks a bit like a 1970s ruffled tuxedo shirt, tends to be the most expensive. It raises horizontally and is usually made of materials like chiffon, satin, or charmeuse.

Continued on p. 54

"I see dead people."
—Cole Sear (Haley Joel Osment),
The Sixth Sense (1999)

The Sixth Sense was reverse-engineered from this line.

Writer-director M. Night Shyamalan had gone to a funeral and saw a boy sitting talking to himself. He mulled over the moment and pondered what the ten-year-old might be saying and thinking. The phrase that came to his mind was "I see dead people."

He began working from there, but according to biographer Michael Bamberger, Shyamalan worried that the phrase sounded too childish for a ten-year-old. He started to convince himself that the line was better suited for someone younger, maybe a six-year-old, and crossed it out.

"And then the voices came," the filmmaker told Bamberger.

Indeed, Shyamalan told the author that "the voices told me to put it back."

"I had faith in the voices," said the man who would earn writing and directing Oscar nominations for his work on the film. "I was just then learning the power of listening to voices."

Knowing the nature of many of Shyamalan's films, like *Wide Awake* and *Lady in the Water*, the filmmaker's connection to the metaphysical makes sense. It also proved to be a good call as the line stuck and helped him crack the plot. Another key move was picking Haley Joel Osment to play the role of the supernaturally gifted Cole Sear.

Shyamalan, who had tested actors from across the nation before meeting Osment, said he knew as soon as the child actor began auditioning he was perfect for the part. (No word on whether any voices helped him with that decision.) In remembering the initial interaction, Osment was low-key about how it all went down. "It just ended up working out," he recalled in 2015. "I guess you could call that my big break."

When it came to shooting the catchphrase that also served as the movie's tagline, Osment remembers the moment with an equally subdued manner.

"When we did that scene, nobody was going, 'That's the line,'" he said. "It was just something that served a very important function in the story."

After the movie proved a surprise hit, grossing more than $670 million worldwide, "I see dead people" attached itself to popular culture. TV shows like *The Simpsons*, *Grey's Anatomy*, and *The Gilmore Girls* all riffed on it. Even into the rise of social media, the dialogue has become a springboard for all sorts of memes such as "I see dumb people" and "I c dead peeps." ★

With that in mind, here's hoping that when your time comes, it's an Austrian rather than a traveler that slowly closes.

Cut to the chase

If you took a time machine back to the first days of filmmaking, the idea of cutting a film would be novel. Original films simply told a story from start to end from one view. It wasn't until 1902 when the pioneering Edwin S. Porter began splicing scenes together with smooth transitions that the concept of elegantly rearranging scenes was put into practice. In the next decade D. W. Griffith improved the practice by adding in a variety of innovations, including long shots and close-ups (see *close-ups*, p. 48).

But as much as the technical elements of *cutting* were being improved, there were some early moviemaking tropes that the industry refused to shake. *Cutting to the chase* was one of them. Before special effects as we know them offered the height of excitement, the chase was the money moment for a cross-section of films from Westerns to the *Keystone Cops* (see p. 96).

The plot point was so common that in 1929 author J. P. McEvoy, who often worked in Hollywood, included it as scene direction in his novel *Hollywood Girl*: "Jannings escapes . . . cut to chase." By the 1940s it had become a tongue-in-cheek law for filmmakers. In 1944 a journalist reported that MGM screenwriter Helen Deutsch posted a sign on her office wall that said "When in doubt, cut to the chase." In 1949 a syndicated columnist told the story of a small New York–based studio that had billboards on its lot reminding everyone of the company's "3 basic rules of movie-making: 'Cut to The Chase,' 'Let The Audience in on the Secret,' and finally 'Better Than Metro Isn't Good Enough.'"

With the expression so commonly used in Hollywood for getting to the good stuff, it entered print as a figure of speech for the same purpose by the 1950s. In 1955 Frank Scully, who knew the movie business

Continued on p. 56

I'll Have Two Movie Stars Straight Up: Drinks with Showbiz Appeal

When it comes to celebrity-named cocktails—whether alcoholic or not—things can get a little hazy. For example, in 1934 a drink named after actress Mary Pickford was said in a syndicated column to include "Italian vermouth, peach brandy [and] gin." But by 1955 another national writer insisted it should have "French vermouth" and threw in some rum and grenadine for good measure (as you'll see below, the concoction has changed yet again today).

Even the story behind the illustrious faux-cocktail the "Shirley Temple" may not be quite what it seems. Legend has it that Temple wanted what the adults were drinking when she went out to dinner one night in Hollywood, and the kid-friendly drink was created to satisfy the young superstar's desires. But in 1988 a sixty-year-old Temple remembered that the famous Hollywood haunt, the Brown Derby, simply named the drink after her and that, for the most part, she couldn't stand her namesake cocktail because it was often made too sweet.

The celebrated New York restaurant-bar the 21 Club baptized a mixed drink called the "Cary Grant" in 1985, but it wasn't necessarily the actor's favorite. He supposedly preferred an unfussy scotch on the rocks in his heyday.

The upshot: Take the following classic movie-star-inspired drinks and their recipes with a grain of salt—or squeeze of lemon or whatever you think will make them work for you—as ingredients (and connections to the stars themselves) do vary.

- Cary Grant: 2 oz. Absolut vodka, a dash of Tio Pepe, and a bit of Rose's lime juice.

- Charlie Chaplin: 1 oz. apricot brandy, 1 oz. sloe gin, 1 oz. fresh lime.
- Douglas Fairbanks: 2 oz. Plymouth gin, 1 oz. dry vermouth.
- Ginger Rogers: 1 oz. dry gin, 1 oz. dry vermouth, 1 oz. apricot brandy, 4 dashes lemon juice.
- Jean Harlow: 2 oz. white rum, 2 oz. sweet vermouth, lemon peel for garnish.
- Marlene Dietrich: 3-4 oz. Canadian whiskey, 2 dashes of Angostura bitters, 2 dashes of Curaçao liqueur.
- Mary Pickford: 2 oz. white rum, 2 oz. pineapple juice, 1 tsp. grenadine, 1 tsp. maraschino liqueur.
- Rosalind Russell: Ice, 2 oz. aquavit, 1 oz. sweet vermouth, 2 dashes Angostura bitters, 1 lemon twist for garnish.
- Roy Rogers: 6-8 oz. cola, $\frac{1}{4}$ oz. grenadine.
- Shirley Temple: 6-8 oz. ginger ale (or lemon-lime soda), dash of grenadine, maraschino cherry.
- Will Rogers: 2 oz. gin, 1 oz. dry vermouth, 1 oz. orange juice, 4 dashes of Curaçao liqueur.

as a regular writer for the industry trade publication *Variety*, applied it figuratively in his autobiography *Cross My Heart*. "I am the sort who wants to 'cut to the chase,'" he wrote. "As far as I'm concerned we can read the instructions later."

Though it was in colloquial use in the following decades, *cut to the chase* gained broad popularity beginning in the late 1980s.

Don't touch that dial

Don't touch that dial is one of those expressions that may soon be forgotten. As talk-show host/comedian Stephen Colbert once joked: "Don't touch that dial. And if your TV has a dial, go buy a new one."

Nevertheless, it's still hanging in there as a figurative way to ask somebody to maintain the course or stay focused on a discussion or task. For example, the *Washington Post* used it in 2013 on a story about the rising stock prices for the media company Discovery Communications. "Some investors might be tempted to sell or avoid it after such a run," the paper said, "but don't touch that dial."

That reference—and all of those before it—can be credited to the opening line of the radio version of the popular comic strip *Blondie*. The show, which lightheartedly told the tale of the couple Blondie and Dagwood Bumstead and ran on various networks between 1939 and 1950, would come on the air to the statement "ah, ah, ah, ah, don't touch that dial. . . ."

The expression immediately became a popular catchphrase. Throughout the 1940s radio stations from Amarillo, Texas, to Zanesville, Ohio, used the expression to convince locals to stick with their programming.

One of the reasons the phrase proved so durable was it neatly fit for two other forms of technology that at one time also required dials: telephones and TVs. In 1941 a store in Syracuse, New York, was one of the first to steal the expression in a telephone sense. "Don't Touch That Dial Again Until You Have Called Meager's Market," it said in an ad it placed in a local newspaper. The line was applied to television in the 1950s.

With dials long gone, the question is how much longer does the phrase (like the similar *stay tuned*—see p. 174) have before it completely fades away? Perhaps it'll prove quite durable. Despite the fact the statement "don't touch that remote" exists, it's never built the same idiomatic cache.

The truth is, sometimes nostalgia does win. After all, while personally penned postal letters are hard to come by anymore, people have yet to replace the seemingly anachronistic *nothing to write home about* with the more up-to-date *nothing to text home about*.

Double take

The origin of this phrase deserves a *double take* of its own. At first glance, *take* appears to come from the early days of film. A *take* was used by 1918 to describe the shooting of a scene. The initial attempt was called *take one*, the second *take two*, and on and on.

If this were the starting point for *double take*, it would be a bit odd. After all, what does filming over and over again have to do with taking a glance at something and then refocusing a second time with surprise? The answer is it doesn't. The world of burlesque and vaudeville coined *take* in this context for a different purpose—as a term of art for a funny reaction.

There were generally four different types of *takes*, according to *The Language of American Popular Entertainment*. One was called the *skull*. It was the "most sudden reaction, usually involving a snap of the head in the direction of the other performer." The next was the *double take*, which like our general usage meant "a somewhat slower realization that things are not as they should be." The third was a *body take*, which was like the *double take* but utilized the entire body in the reaction rather than just the head. The final option was the *slow take*, which was a deeply delayed reaction.

The *double take* was a humorous staple by the time early comedies were being filmed. When actress Alice Brady was learning the art of the *double take* in 1937, the *Washington Post* described it as one of "the old comedy tricks of [pioneering comedy filmmaker] Mack Sennett vintage." (See *Keystone Cops*, p. 96, for more on Sennett.)

That said, even after the expression had taken root, it was not universally used in Hollywood. For instance, in a 1936 newspaper article, Charley Rogers, who wrote for the comedy duo Laurel and Hardy, described this tool as a "take 'em."

"There are innumerable variations of the 'take 'em' and no limit on the number that can be done in sequence," the story explained. "[Actor] Harry Langdon has been known to do as many as 20."

Thankfully, the *twenty take* never took linguistic hold. Instead, nonactors were said to be doing *double takes* when surprised by at least the 1950s. Another expression with a similar lineage, *deadpan* crossed over around the same time. *Deadpan* for an emotionally blank look (with *pan* being slang for a face) was also an early tool in a vaudeville or burlesque actor's arsenal.

Drama queen

Being a *drama queen* was once a badge of honor. The expression's earliest known example in print is from 1923 when the editor of *House and Garden* argued in the *Washington Post* that every man deserved a relaxation room to himself. "If he is thwarted in his effort . . . he may either go to the dogs or the drama queens, become short-tempered, sullen, grouchy and eventually feel that in a way he is a failure," the journalist wrote.

While that stray reference might suggest the modern *drama queen* meaning of someone prone to overreact, it appears to be an anomaly, because for much of the middle half of the twentieth century, the term was innocently used to describe a talented actress. In advertising for the 1937 film *The Emperor's Candlesticks*, Luise Rainer, who had won the best actress Oscar the previous year for her work in *The Great Ziegfeld*, was pumped up as the "Academy drama queen."

For the most part in this period, the phrase was also used literally for teenagers who had received accolades as top theatrical performers—much like there were homecoming queens, there were also *drama queens*. An example: A 1955 feature on a young Shirley Jones (who would go on to win a supporting actress Academy Award in 1961 for *Elmer Gantry* and play the mom in TV's *The Partridge Family*) pointed out that while in high school in Niagara Falls, New York, Jones was "a majorette of the school band, soloist in the glee club, honor student and star drama queen."

Continued on p. 62

> ## "If you build it, he will come."
> ## —The Voice (Himself),
> ## *Field of Dreams* (1989)

Generally speaking, when an actor delivers a culturally meaningful line in a movie, the performer wants to take credit for it. Heck, director Rob Reiner was so thrilled that *his mother*, Estelle, produced the wisecrack "I'll have what she's having" in *When Harry Met Sally . . .*, following Meg Ryan's ersatz orgasm at a deli, that he's proudly discussed it in more than one interview. (*Geek note*: Reiner's mom wasn't supposed to be in the film, coming to the set that day just to see her son before shining in the walk-on role.)

But when it comes to "if you build it, he will come," which is often misquoted as "if you build it, they will come," nobody (as of 2016) has officially stood up and claimed ownership for vocalizing those words. In the movie's closing credits, the role of the "the Voice" was cryptically said to have been played by "Himself."

For years, there were rumors about who that might be. Two of the movie's stars, Ray Liotta and Kevin Costner, were mentioned. (When the American Film Institute put out a list of the top four hundred movie quotes of all time in 2005, it credited Liotta with the statement.) Nevertheless, twenty-five years after the film's release, W. P. Kinsella, who originally wrote the famous line for the picture's underlying source material, the book *Shoeless Joe*, gave us the closest thing to a proper attribution.

Kinsella said he was "told that the Voice that speaks to Ray [Kevin Costner] in the cornfield was, though not credited, Ed Harris." This revelation was certainly plausible as the four-time Oscar nominee did have a connection to the film through his wife Amy Madigan, who co-starred in the movie.

While the filmmakers clearly wanted to preserve the anonymous other-worldly quality of the Voice, the line did cause some real-world problems.

Field of Dreams was shot in Dyersville, Iowa, and the year the movie was filmed, the area was suffering through a drought. This created a hitch because the screenplay required that when Costner first hears "if you build it, he will come" in the cornfield, the stalks had to be as tall as the actor.

"What happened was they had to have shots of the corn being little and then growing bigger," said Dwier Brown, who played Costner's father, John, in the movie. "Well, it came to that time in the shoot [for the voice] and the corn was two feet tall."

Production was stopped while they irrigated the land enough to get the corn to around six feet.

"You have the big old Mississippi coming out of there, this giant river and yet no one a mile off it could get any water, at least, the kind of water that didn't render their crop neutral," Costner recounted. "All the farmers were having a very bad crop season and here we are, we're Hollywood and we're watering the corn. It looked bizarre and also felt very selfish."

While in movie terms this line is relatively young (compare it to many others in this book), it's still one that has a vintage quality. In 2009 Kathie Lee Gifford referenced it on the *Today* show and was already calling it an "old saying." ★

According to *Cassell's Dictionary of Slang*, the expression transitioned to its snarkier definition in the 1960s via the gay community. But it wasn't until the 1970s that this meaning began getting traction in general print. For the record, one of the first *drama queens* of this nature appears to have been a character on *The New Dick Van Dyke Show*. Barbara Rush, who had a long feature career starring opposite the likes of Paul Newman, Richard Burton, and Kirk Douglas, played the recurring role of diva Margot Brighton. TV listings that ran throughout American papers in October 1973 said the actress would appear on an episode as the "daytime drama queen Margot Brighton, who becomes enraged at both Dick and Jenny when a gossip columnist reports that Dick said, 'She kisses like a dead mackerel.'"

The phrase's popularity really began to blow up in the 1990s, when everyone from Madonna to Angela Bassett self-identified in interviews as *drama queens*. Nowadays, when applying the title, gender really doesn't matter.

"He's a drama queen," said former coach Jimmy Johnson about quarterback Brett Favre in 2010. "While some of his ailments are real, and he's got some problems, there's no doubt about that, but he loves to play it up, he loves the spotlight."

Dress rehearsal

Theatrical *rehearsals* long predate the actual creation of an English word for the activity. The Greek historian Plutarch, for example, wrote about Euripides (circa 480 BC–470 BC) getting frustrated with another actor who laughed while he was rehearsing a serious speech.

In our language the stage took the word *rehearsal* to represent practicing a play or other production by the 1500s. It was originally in circulation around 1400 when Chaucer used it to generally reflect recounting, reciting, or repeating something previously written or heard.

While the term *rehearsal* was borrowed, a *dress rehearsal* was a true theatrical creation. Writers were mentioning both *dress rehearsals* and *dressed rehearsals* as the final practice before regular stage performances in the 1700s. Still, its existence could be older if you take into account the longer history of the word *rehearsal* and the fact that *dress* (to mean clothing for a special function) can be found in the 1600s. In America the expression seems to have taken a little longer to become entrenched. In 1852 the *New York Times* ran an article about how their music critic covered a "dress rehearsal" for a new production. Along with that mention was a question from another paper, the *Evening Mirror*, asking "Will [the critic] be kind enough to explain what he means by a 'dress rehearsal'?"

Around that time the British had already adapted the phrase for figurative use. In 1868, for example, the leading satirical publication *Punch* featured a cartoon of a newly named minister in full uniform admiring himself a mirror with the caption "A dress rehearsal." American publications began using it metaphorically near the end of the 1800s, which also happened to be a period when actual theatrical *dress rehearsals* were getting maligned in the media on both sides of the Atlantic.

"A dress rehearsal is rather amusing to the idler who strolls into the stalls, but to the actor it is simply horrible," explained a London magazine called *Temple Bar* in 1883. "The company is very tired of rehearsals, and quite spiritless. . . . One feels feverish and unreal, it is difficult to rouse oneself into the right mood and deliver a speech with spirit."

It was no different in the United States. "The dress rehearsal is more dreaded by actors than the first public performance," proclaimed the American publication *Frank Leslie's Popular Monthly* in 1893. "Throughout each act there is a deadly silence in the auditorium; the funniest lines never get as much as a smile; every man appears an enemy, and each scene is frequently interrupted by both author and manager."

Fade-out

The *fade-out* (and *fade-in*) were created at the dawn of Hollywood, and according to an early book on filmmaking, they were initially part of a cheap batch of gimmicks created to keep audiences coming back.

Continued on p. 66

"I'll be back."
—Terminator (Arnold Schwarzenegger), *The Terminator* (1984)

The first time he was asked, Arnold Schwarzenegger was adamant: He didn't want to say this signature catchphrase. In fact, the actor described his effort to alter the line as "the biggest disagreement" he had with writer-director James Cameron while shooting the original *Terminator* movie.

In his autobiography *Total Recall*, Schwarzenegger explained that his hang-up was specifically with the word *I'll*.

"I felt that the line would sound more machinelike and menacing without the contraction," he wrote. "'It's feminine when I say the *I'll*,' I complained, repeating it for Jim [Cameron] so he could hear the problem. 'I'll. I'll. I'll.' It doesn't feel rugged to me."

The future California governor attributed his stance, in part, to a bit of a cultural divide. "The truth was that, even after all these years of speaking English," he said, "I still didn't understand contractions."

For his part, Cameron brushed off the star's requests to deadpan "I will be back," saying, according to Schwarzenegger's book: "Look, just trust me, okay? I don't tell you how to act, and you don't tell me how to write."

After the movie was released in the fall of 1984, Schwarzenegger was caught off-guard by how well the line was received. When he returned to the United States following another shoot abroad, the actor was stopped on a New York street by a group and was begged to "say it!" Schwarzenegger had to ask what exactly they wanted him to say.

From there, he learned the value of embracing dialogue. When "Hasta la vista, baby," showed up in his script for *Terminator 2: Judgment Day*, he didn't hesitate, saying it was a key moment that "humanized" his cyborg character.

As for "I'll be back," despite his protests during the filming, the phrase became a centerpiece in both his film and political careers. For example, he used the line in movies as varied as the actioner *Commando* and the light comedy *Twins*. (*Geek note*: It also shows up in one form or another in all five of the *Terminator* movies; though another character uses it in 2009's *Terminator Salvation*.)

During the 2003 gubernatorial recall election, "I'll be back" became a Schwarzenegger campaign slogan, and "the Governor" didn't stop there, wielding it countless times during his tenure—from supporting a series of controversial ballot initiatives to touting California products in Japan. ★

Author and sometime screenwriter Homer Croy wrote in his 1918 book *How Motion Pictures Are Made* that so many of the early cinematic manipulations—like cutting film so a princess could magically disappear—were what he called "trick pictures." While he sounded like a man ahead of his time, he believed that an overdose of these special effects underestimated the audience.

"It was not yet realized that an audience would be content to sit and watch the gradual unfolding of a plot with the consequent crossing of purpose and clash of will of the characters involved," Croy wrote.

Fade-outs and *fade-ins* initially fell into this category. But Croy did allow that there was ultimately artistic merit in slowing shifting to or from a black screen to enhance drama, known collectively as *fading*.

"Experimenting only to mystify audiences, new and valuable camera methods were discovered which have come to be used more and more in accepted [film] photography," he wrote. "A fade-in might show a splotch of high light which slowly takes on detail until it is seen that it is moonlight on a girl's hair and then as the details grow more distinct the girl is seen sitting in a French window, her chin on her hand waiting for her lover."

Croy was not alone in recognizing the long-term merit of this practice, as so many directors, including superstars like D. W. Griffith, used *fading*.

As a piece of general language, those outside the industry were offering up the term figuratively by the 1920s. Generally, *fade-out* to describe love, career, or, ultimately, life slipping away was the more popular construction. The satiric British publication *Punch* used it in a 1928 story: "The veriest front-row flapper knows that marriage is the 'fade-out' of love." The comparable *fade to black* took on a similar idiomatic meaning later, though its roots appear to be connected to the stage, where it was used in the direction "lights fade to black."

Technically, there were four initial ways to create the desired *fade-in/fade-out* effect. The first was closing or opening the diaphragm of the lens. Two other mechanical options were "dissolving the shutter," in which a blade slowly passed over the shutter in the camera until it was totally covered; and using a "graduated screen" to achieve the same goal but with a strip of glass over the lens. A final option: treating the developed film with chemicals after the shoot. (*Geek note*: The term *dissolve* also existed for this process, but its metaphorical popularity for instances like "dissolving a marriage" far predated the movie use.)

Of course, current filmmakers primarily rely on digital technology, so all of this is now typically done on a computer. One can only wonder what Croy would have said about the "tricks" created by those machines.

Flashback

The early history of *flashbacks* is about as unclear as the gauzy fades used in movies to switch from the present to these scenes of the past.

While historians are certain that pioneering filmmakers created this technique, they aren't sure who first innovated it. The reason: Many movies from the time are lost, as most of the actual celluloid didn't survive the period. What we do know is during the first decade of the 1900s, it was common to superimpose a small picture to represent dream sequences and, likely, to a lesser extent, memories of the past. Think of it as a similar setup for FaceTime on the iPhone (the little picture of you in the corner is where the *flashback* went). According to historian Barry Salt, the earliest known surviving *flashback* in this style comes from a 1904 silent film called *The Old Chorister*. By 1909 *flashbacks* were getting full-screen treatment in stand-alone scenes in pictures like *Napoleon, the Man of Destiny*.

Another issue impacting our understanding of it all was that early moviemaking language wasn't always well defined. At the time, people were using terms for similar-sounding technology like *cutbacks* and *switchbacks*. The question was: What did it all mean? Director D. W. Griffith appears to have used those words interchangeably for something other than what we understand as a *flashback*. These types of shots were what we now refer to as cutting between two scenes happening at the same time. So, when Griffith took credit for coming up with the "switch-back" in a 1911 ad, it muddled the point as it's likely he came up with switching between same-time, different-location scenes but didn't devise backward-looking storytelling.

Even beyond Griffith, there was other confusion. In 1916 *Variety* mentioned *flashbacks* in our modern way, but the following year a book called *How to Write for Moving Pictures* (1917) used it and the term *dissolve* interchangeably, according to historian Maureen Turim. For most, even at that time, a *dissolve* was what we'd call a *fade-out* (see p. 63).

Despite all the bewilderment, the concept of *flashbacks* and the word used for it were crystal-clear by the 1920s. In the following decade the term was employed in a wider sense for recollecting the past even when not on the silver screen.

Gangbusters

J. Edgar Hoover deserves credit—and infamy—for many things during his forty-eight-year tenure as director of the FBI. But one little-discussed contribution to language was his indirect role in making *gangbusters* an idiom-worthy word.

The term, which can mean either achieving great success ("iPads are selling like gangbusters") or acting with vigor ("the football team came out like gangbusters, scoring on its first drive"), was originally coined for a more literal purpose: to describe hard-charging cops in the 1930s who broke up organized-crime syndicates.

In 1935 the word was likely known to radio producer Phillips Lord when he was devising a new show that would focus on the work of the FBI. However, at first he didn't use it because he got Hoover's cooperation to work closely with the FBI. That allowed him to go with a built-in title for his program: *G-Men*.

Lord would learn quickly that people generally didn't work *with* Hoover but *for* the man. The FBI director made numerous demands on the production. In particular, he reportedly didn't want *G-Men* to focus on the gunplay but rather the boring tick-tock process that his investigators had to go through to crack a case.

After one thirteen-episode season, the two men dissolved their collaboration. Without Hoover, sponsor Chevrolet pulled out and its NBC network dropped the show. Lord had to come up with a new program—and a different name.

Enter *Gang Busters*. Debuting on CBS in 1936, the retitled show (thank you, Mr. Hoover) became tremendously popular. It was not only a radio favorite until 1957, but it also led to a TV series—as well as movie serials and comic books—of the same name. The franchise status it enjoyed surely contributed to *gangbusters'* idiomatic usage for a great success.

But why the connection between the show and the metaphorical definition of an initial burst of energy as in *coming on* (or *out*) *like gangbusters*?

It all had to with the beginning of broadcasts. *Gang Busters* started with sirens, gunfire, and whistles, among other startling sound effects, and then went directly into their stories, which were billed as "the only national program that brings you authentic police cases."

By the 1940s that show's popularity and the excitement the opening brought led to the title becoming popular shorthand for listeners on matters well beyond the show.

Gaslight (gaslighting)

Have you ever had that horrible feeling that the details of your life are slightly off and that maybe somebody in your world is manipulating them to make you go crazy? If so, you're not alone—it happened to Ingrid Bergman. Okay, it didn't really happen to the great actress but

Continued on p. 72

> ## "I'm as mad as hell and I'm not going to take this anymore."
> ## —Howard Beale (Peter Finch), *Network* (1976)

Just before *Network* came out, Paddy Chayefsky, who won an Oscar for its screenplay, insisted he really wasn't as mad as hell as some people thought.

Iconic newswoman Barbara Walters laid into the movie just weeks before its release, calling its portrayal of TV network news "unfair" and suggesting that Chayefsky, who had much success as a TV writer, experienced "bitterness" toward the industry.

Chayefsky responded by saying he hadn't intended to do a "hatchet job" in this satiric movie about an anchorman going crazy on air. "To me," he said, "television is a symptom of something awful that could turn into something worse.... I've never had any bitter experiences in television. All the people in television I've talked to love the picture. Of course, unless it's a big kiss on the you-know-what, some people will take offense."

Indeed, at the time, not everyone in the broadcast news business was mad as hell either. CBS's famed anchor Walter Cronkite said he found the movie "rather amusing" and John Chancellor, who anchored *NBC Nightly News*, described the film as "pretty funny."

For actor Peter Finch, who delivered the "I'm as mad as hell and I'm not going to take this anymore!" line, it was a difficult speech to pull off. The monologue was shot two ways. One was on videotape so there could be cuts to the control room and home screens across the country, and the other was a master shot that would show Finch's character, Howard Beale, in the studio.

When it came to filming the master shot, Finch could only muster one full take and half of a second one.

"Between the length of the speech and the amount of emotion it took, he just ran out of gas," director Sidney Lumet said in the book *Mad as Hell: The Making of* Network *and the Fateful Vision of the Angriest Man in Movies*. "He stopped halfway through. He said, 'Sidney, I can't do any more.'"

Finch's inability to offer more takes changed how this line came out on the screen. The script read "I'm mad as hell," but Finch shifted it ever so slightly to "I'm as mad as hell." Since Finch only uttered the words once for the master shot, there was no way to fix it.

No matter, most people today still remember it without the extra "as," and the change certainly didn't diminish the catchphrase's immediate impact.

On January 13, less than two months after the movie's release, Johnny Carson interviewed Finch on *The Tonight Show*. The host would gush: "There are certain lines from motion pictures that you always remember. That's the one."

"Well, I'm . . . I'm very lucky, I suppose," Finch responded, "because people go around quoting it. And if an actor's associated with one of those lines, it gives you a lot of . . ." but Carson cut him off before he could finish.

Finch would die of a heart attack the following morning, and on March 28 would become the first actor to win a posthumous Academy Award. ★

to a character she played, which, in turn, gave rise to *gaslighting*, a psychological term for subtly undermining a person's sense of reality in an attempt to make that individual lose his or her mind.

Fittingly, the 1944 film in question was called *Gaslight*, and it starred Bergman and Charles Boyer as her husband. The movie, which was based on a play that ran in England and then on Broadway, featured Boyer deviously trying to crush Bergman's psyche by, among other acts, flickering the gaslights in their house and then claiming it wasn't occurring.

While the play, which was called *Angel Street* in the United States, had its supporters, this movie's success—it earned Bergman her first of three Oscars—almost certainly inspired the term *gaslighting*. (*Geek note*: A British film adaptation of the stage drama was released in 1940, but MGM bought the remake rights to do the Boyer-Bergman movie and insisted that all the prints from the earlier version be destroyed; some survived that recall, but it limited that version's cultural impact.)

At first, the idea of *gaslighting* was picked up for benign purposes. Beginning in the 1950s, TV sitcom writers named scenarios where one character was fooling another as the *gaslight treatment* or the *gaslight bit*. Programs like *The George Burns and Gracie Allen Show*, *Car 54, Where are You?* and *Make Room for Daddy* all used the *gaslight treatment* to comedic effect.

But by the 1960s the expression had taken on a more serious tone in psychology circles. In a 1969 book called *Changing Perspectives in Mental Illness*, the author wrote: "It is . . . popularly believed to be possible to 'gaslight' a perfectly healthy person into psychosis by interpreting his own behavior to him as symptomatic of serious mental illness."

Beyond *gaslighting*, Hollywood continues to this day to play a role in offering language metaphors for nefarious misdirection with the word *catfish*. The title of the 2010 documentary *Catfish* gave us that term (as a noun or verb) to describe a person who sets up a fraudulent online persona to romantically entrap another. In the documen-

Continued on p. 75

All The World's a Stage: Shakespeare's Linguistic Contributions

Any argument questioning the impact of theater on the English language can be shut down with two words: William Shakespeare. The Bard of Avon's contributions to the way we speak could fill a book of its own. According to eminent Victorian language expert F. Max Müller, Shakespeare used approximately fifteen thousand different words in his plays; the *Oxford English Dictionary* gives him credit for coining about two thousand of them (though that number has dwindled over the years as earlier sources have been found for some originally attributed to him). Still, what's so astonishing is we continue to rely on scores of them more than four hundred years after he first penned his works. As a refresher, here are some (but nowhere near all) of the well-known idioms and phrases believed to be coined by Shakespeare along with the plays they can be found in and their modern-day figurative meanings.

- "All that glisters [glitters] is not gold" (*Merchant of Venice*): Some things that superficially appear valuable are worthless.
- "Bated breath" (*Merchant of Venice*): Acting with anticipation, excitement (or fear).
- "Be-all, end-all" (*Macbeth*): The most important thing or moment.
- "Comedy of errors" (*Comedy of Errors*): An astoundingly long (and therefore laughable) series of mistakes.
- "Discretion is the better part of valor" (*Henry IV, Part I*): Using caution before entering a dangerous situation is a good idea.
- "Eaten out of house and home" (*Henry IV, Part II*): To have everything (primarily food) taken.

- "Fancy-free" (*Midsummer Night Dream*): To be unshackled by commitment.
- "For goodness' sake" (*Henry VIII*): An exclamation of frustration.
- "A foregone conclusion" (*Othello*): An opinion that's been formed before all the evidence is clear.
- "Give the devil his due" (*Henry IV, Part I*): To pay a debt (or respect) to a disreputable person.
- "Green-eyed monster" (*Othello*): Jealousy.
- "Heart of heart[s]" (*Hamlet*): One's innermost feelings.
- "Heart's content" (*Merchant of Venice*): Being fully satisfied.
- "Hot-blooded" (*Merry Wives of Windsor*): Deeply passionate or hot-tempered.
- "It was Greek to me" (*Julius Caesar*): Not understanding what another is saying or what is written.
- "Lily-livered" (*Macbeth*): Cowardly.
- "One fell swoop" (*Macbeth*): Done in a single action.
- "A plague on both your houses" (*Romeo and Juliet*): A curse on both sides of a dispute.
- "A pound of flesh" (*Merchant of Venice*): An unfair or absurdly high payment that is required.
- "Primrose path" (*Hamlet*): The seemingly easy course in life (that can prove disastrous).
- "Salad days" (*Antony and Cleopatra*): That wonderful period of youth; youthful inexperience.
- "Short shrift" (*Richard III*): To give little attention to; to make cursory work of an activity.
- "Star-crossed lovers" (*Romeo and Juliet*): Lovers with a tragic fate.
- "There's the rub" (*Hamlet*): There is a problem or difficulty.
- "[Vanish] into thin air" (*The Tempest*): To disappear.

tary, one of the subjects, who had been duped online, philosophically likened his experience to being a cod transported by sea for sale. He explained that cod were kept agile by catfish who were shipped with them on long voyages. These nipping catfish apparently made the otherwise lazy cod edible at the end of the long journey. Though the story, which some suggest was based on an older Christian parable, doesn't appear to be historically accurate (and only vaguely—if even that—related to the modern meaning), the term was taken by MTV for a reality show about online dating ruses, which threw *catfish* in this sense into the vernacular.

Get out of Dodge

Gunsmoke was an American institution. The Western aired on television from 1955 to 1975 and remains the longest-running prime-time live-action drama in TV history. With such a lengthy run on the cultural stage, it figures it would also find a place in our linguistic psyche.

The show's hero, Marshall Matt Dillon (played by Jim Arness), was the law in Dodge City, Kansas. As was the case in real life during the 1880s, the fictional Dodge in the program was a crossroads of cowboys, criminals, and townsfolk. So when the bad guys started stirring up trouble, Arness often gave them the ultimatum: "Get out of Dodge." The command usually also came with a timetable (like leave town within twenty-four hours).

By the 1960s journalists were referencing this decree. In a 1960 article nationally syndicated columnist Jack Smith pondered a newfangled invention: the tape recorder. The story juxtaposed the great statements that could now be saved as oral history with the banal words of television. One phrase he included: "Mister . . . you better get out of Dodge." Four years later, the expression was so well known that a *Las Vegas Sun* editor used the headline "Get Out of Dodge, Ma'am" for an article on two women in New Mexico running for local sheriff positions.

In terms of going idiomatic, *get out of Dodge* crossed over, in part, because of the type of guys that Marshall Dillon would have wanted to kick out of his town.

In 1965 a judge named Joseph L. McGlynn Jr. was overseeing a West Philadelphia gang-shooting trial. He was struggling to understand the slang the teenagers testifying were using so he asked the Juvenile Aid Division of the Philadelphia County Court to translate. Among the phrases, he learned *get out of Dodge* was being used as a euphemism for "lay low."

Everyday usages for the expression continued to develop over the next decade. In 1973 a newspaper reported on graffiti found in a tough, predominantly African-America area of San Francisco, urging white prostitutes to leave the neighborhood. "White tricks go home . . . Leave our black women alone . . . get out of Dodge," it said.

From there the phrase went mainstream, generally meaning to leave (often quickly). The hardscrabble colloquial roots also probably influenced two popular variations: *get the heck out of Dodge* and *get the hell out of Dodge.*

Get the hook

It probably shouldn't come as a surprise that the phrases *get the hook* and *amateur night* are so closely related. The first person to *get the hook* was a less-than-spectacular singer who had taken to the stage at Miner's Bowery Theater in New York, according to a 1908 book called *Get the Hook.*

Here's how it went down: In 1903 the theater's proprietor, Thomas Miner, began the practice of letting neophytes perform on Friday nights. These proto–*America's Got Talent* events, which would soon be called *amateur nights*, were greeted with a mixed bag of emotions by the audience. (*Geek note*: *Amateur night* would become idiomatic for ineptitude by the 1930s.) For the good acts, people would throw money on the stage. But when someone was terrible, the audience would let them have it.

On one particular October night that year, an aspiring singer with "an impossible (near) tenor voice" wouldn't leave the stage despite all forms of verbal abuse. Miner realized he'd have to resort to extreme measures before the crowd totally got out of hand. He saw an "old fashioned crook handled cane" and secured it to a pole to give it length. "With this he stepped to the wings and without getting in sight of the audience deftly slipped the hook around the neck of the would-be singer and yanked him off the stage before he really knew what had happened," according to the book.

When the singer was followed by an actor doing the "worst imaginable" dramatic speech, a boy in the gallery yelled, "Get the hook!" and from there the grand theater tradition began.

While the retelling has an air of drama that could cast some doubt on its reliability, the tale was generally accepted. When Miner died in 1928 at the age of fifty-eight, his obituary focused on how he "gave the amusement world that enduring battle cry 'Get the hook!'"

Assuming the expression got its start on that fateful 1903 evening, it moved quickly into nationwide prominence. Within a couple of years, baseball fans were using it to suggest pulling an underperforming player (or umpire) from a game. It also made its mark in politics.

At the 1908 Republican Presidential Convention, Indiana Governor Frank Hanly took the podium to voice support for his fellow Hoosier (and wannabe presidential candidate) Vice President Charles Fairbanks. Proving that you don't have to be an amateur to *get the hook*, a report in the *Rockford Democrat* (Illinois) said that when Hanly made covertly critical comments about outgoing president Teddy Roosevelt, "bedlam broke loose" as those on the floor began yelling "Get the hook, hook, hook!"

Going off-script

If you think calling a Hollywood writer's work a *screenplay* instead of a *script* is using the terminology cinema's inventors intended, guess again.

Continued on p. 80

> ## "I'm gonna make him an offer he can't refuse."
> ### —Don Vito Corleone (Marlon Brando), *The Godfather* (1972)

This phrase—and *The Godfather*, in general—would have never happened if author Mario Puzo got his way back in 1965. He'd penned the critically well-received *Fortunate Pilgrim* and wanted to write another similar piece. He didn't think a mafia opera was it. Still, he was in debt, so he did it, admitting just before the movie was released: "I wrote [the book] to make money."

The decision worked out as the novel became a runaway best-seller. When it came to writing the script, the final draft was a collaboration between Puzo and director Francis Ford Coppola. (They would share an Oscar for their work.)

"He rewrote one half and I rewrote the second half," Puzo said. "Then we traded and rewrote each other. I suggested we work together. Francis looked me right in the eye and said no. That's when I knew he was really a director."

Despite all the changes, Don Corleone's "offer" was an element that came from Puzo's book. The scene in the film in which Don Corleone promises to make sure a Hollywood producer gives singer Tony Fontana a part he desires is structured slightly differently than the novel, but the line was generally preserved. The book says "He's a businessman. . . . I'll make him an offer he can't refuse," while the film has it as "I'm gonna make him an offer he can't refuse."

Puzo and Coppola must have known they had something good as the phrase shows up multiple times in the film and its two sequels.

The etymology website The Phrase Finder (www.phrases.org.uk) points out that this expression wasn't new to the movies. In the 1934 film *Burn 'Em Up Barnes*, a character played by Jason Robards Sr. says, "I'll make her an offer she can't refuse." But the website adds that it was the intention of Marlon Brando's line that made it so long-lasting as a catchphrase.

"The [Robards] character is suggesting making a large and tempting offer of cash—it is meant to be taken as generosity rather than a threat," The Phrase Finder article said. In contrast, "the *Godfather* character could ironically pretend that his 'offer' was benevolent." (If somehow you haven't seen the movie, let's just say there was nothing kind about Don Corleone's hardball approach.)

Despite all the adulation Puzo received for his work, years after the first two *Godfather* films, he still lamented about his book: "I'd always wish[ed] I'd written it better." ★

Consider the January 1912 issue of the *Moving Picture News*, an early film industry periodical. The magazine makes more than two dozen references to *scripts* being used by studios and not one mention of a *screenplay*.

This is because, linguistically speaking, the *script* came first. A *script* was short for *manuscript*, which became a term for a document by at least the 1600s. This connection was made clear in a 1918 book called *How Motion Pictures Are Made*. "The story as it arrives in manuscript form at the studio is told in as few words as possible," author Homer Croy wrote. "On its acceptance a working script is made from the story."

A cynical explanation for why *script* was chosen came from a 1928 edition of the language journal *American Speech*. "'Script,' in my opinion is a gift of the free-lance hack-writer, who always prefers 'manuscript' to the salaried newspaperman's 'copy,'" wrote an academic named Albert Parry.

No matter, *script* was adopted. In contrast, *screenplay* was initially contemplated for a different purpose. In the trailblazing days of the film business, moviemakers weren't sure what to call their onscreen product. Some referred to them as *moving pictures* and others called them *movies* or *motion pictures*. One studio, the Essanay Company, even held a contest to give their product a more elegant name. (The winner was *photoplay*, which didn't get much momentum other than to be taken as the name of a popular fan magazine.) Among those options used was the word *screenplay*. In a 1916 advertisement Metro Pictures used it, calling *Romeo and Juliet* "the screen play of the year"—and they weren't talking about the *script*. As we all know, *screenplay* didn't make the cut in that fashion but was given the consolation prize of being a fancy way to say *script*.

Notwithstanding the *script*'s founding history, it took a long time for the word to get reshaped for figurative uses. Calling an obviously planned action *scripted* or going the other direction and describing a moment of improvisation as *going off-script* didn't catch on until after World War II.

While it took a while, the *script* certainly won out as an idiomatic touchstone compared to the *screenplay*. You've got to admit, it wouldn't sound that good if when contemplating making a last-minute change to your plans, you said, "I'm thinking about *going off-screenplay*."

Groundhog Day

Movie titles have a long history of serving as placeholders in language. The 1933 film *King Kong* became synonymous for a big burly guy, and *Animal House* (1978) is sometimes used to describe any sort of debauched party central (or just messy) locale (also, see *Gaslighting*, p. 69). But *Groundhog Day* may take the film-name award for being recast into such a popular expression.

For those of you without a deep appreciation for comedy classics (shame on you), *Groundhog Day* told the story of a Pittsburgh weatherman named Phil Connors (Bill Murray). He goes to the town of Punxsutawney, Pennsylvania, to cover the annual Groundhog Day festivities but gets stuck in a time loop, reliving the same day over and over again.

The movie was a solid success when it came out in 1993, but it earned cult status over the years. So much so that decades after its release, everyone from Britney Spears to the panel on the long-running political show *Meet the Press* have invoked it in recent years for situations that continued to repeat themselves.

Why did Groundhog Day—rather than, say, Arbor Day—earn this linguistic honor? It was primarily happenstance, according to the film's co-writer Danny Rubin. He'd come up with the idea for the film in late January and picked up a calendar to brainstorm which day should serve as the centerpiece for the plot.

"The first holiday I came to was two days later, Groundhog Day, and I was thinking about that, saying, 'Well, this is perfect. It's a completely unexploited holiday. We can play it on TV every year like the Charlie Brown specials," Rubin joked. But as he mapped out how a weatherman would be forced to be in "unfamiliar territory" to cover the groundhog event away from "family and friends . . . a bunch of things just started falling together."

The bigger question, of course, is when you're caught in a *Groundhog Day*–like cycle, how long will it last? In terms of the length of time in the movie, it's been a much-debated topic. One Internet writer crunched the numbers and claimed it would be a minimum of eight years, eight months, and sixteen days. Another person (with clearly lots of time on his hands) wrote that Murray was in this limbo state for thirty-three years and 358 days.

For his part, the film's director and co-writer Harold Ramis spoke twice on this matter. In a DVD commentary, he initially estimated that Murray was stuck on the same day for about ten years. But after all the Internet hubbub, he recalculated.

"I think the 10-year estimate is too short," he e-mailed to one of the bloggers who wrote on the topic in 2009. "It takes at least 10 years to get good at anything, and allotting for down time and misguided years he spent, it had to be more like 30 or 40 years."

Ham (hamming it up)

This porcine-inspired term for an overtly attention-seeking person comes from the strange-sounding word *hamfatter*.

In the nineteenth century actors who couldn't afford fine oils would be forced to slather their faces with pork lard known as *hamfatter* in order to properly apply colored powders. Since it typically tracked that if you couldn't pay for high-end materials, you were likely a lesser light on the stage, *hamfatter*, which was shortened to *ham actor* or simply *ham* by 1882, became a synonym for an amateurish (or over-the-top) performer.

While that explanation is quite tidy, others have offered up alternative starting points. One begins with a then-well-known African-American minstrel song called *The Ham Fat Man*. This tune was a popular choice for auditions, leading producers to allegedly call those who picked it *hamfatters*. Of course, if this one isn't exactly true, it is possible that the song just gave us *hamfatter*, which was then co-opted by actors for makeup.

On the other hand, the renowned journalist H. L. Mencken, who was a bit of a ham himself, proposed that the term was short for William Shakespeare's eponymous character in *Hamlet*, because actors would do whatever it took (including heavy-handed acting) to gain great applause in the title role.

Others say this idiom came from an act produced by Tony Pastor, who ran a New York vaudeville house beginning in 1865. Among his performers was a group called the Hamtown Students, a quartet of black-face actors renowned for their "exaggerated movements and the overblown nature of their act," according to *The Language of American Popular Entertainment*. That book adds that Pastor figures in another option. His theater supposedly had regular ham giveaways on Mondays, leading wags to playfully call his employees *ham actors*.

Alternatively, there was a touring troupe in the mid- to late 1800s run by a guy named Hamish McCullough, who may have lent his nickname, Ham, for this purpose. Even though all signs point to this term being an American creation, some have even claimed it comes from a gaudily decorated mansion called Ham House, which is located near the London suburb of Richmond.

All that said, the connection between *hamfatter*—whatever that word's starting point—and *ham actor* is most likely. A lighthearted story that ran in an 1889 edition of the *Oak Park Reporter* (Illinois) supports this tie. A character in the little piece of fiction describes a fellow thespian as ". . . a ham. Regular hamfatter."

Assuming the *hamfatter* beginning is accurate, those people who offered up fanciful alternative birthing stories have been, to use the expression the term spawned, just *hamming it up*. Calling someone a *ham* outside of the theater came into use before the midpoint of the twentieth century.

"I'm the king of the world!"
—Jack Dawson (Leonardo DiCaprio), *Titanic* (1997)

Filmmaker James Cameron once described a script as "a dynamic document." After what he called "the bones of a good scene," he said, he liked "to play with it and see what else it can yield."

Such was the case with this memorable moment in *Titanic*.

While moviegoers saw Leonardo DiCaprio hanging on the bow of the *Titanic* yelling these words, the actor actually did it on a soundstage in front of a green screen with a fan blowing in his and co-star Danny Nucci's faces. The beauty around them would be digitized later, but when shooting, Cameron was perched on a crane about a hundred feet from the actors with the camera, which was swooping around to give the illusion that they were actually on a moving ship.

"I'm the king of the world" wasn't in the script. Still, Cameron wanted DiCaprio to say something at this early moment of euphoria so the director started making suggestions.

"Jim even had Leo howl like a wolf at one point," Oscar-winning *Titanic* producer Jon Landau said. "Jim didn't feel anything they had tried felt right. Then Jim told Leo to try 'I'm the king of the world.' Leo said, 'Really?' He was pretty skeptical. Jim said, 'Yeah, Jack feels like he's the king of the world, even though he's the king of nothing. . . . It's an irony.' Leo tried it and Jim liked it best of what they tried and we moved on."

According to Landau, Cameron came up with the line on the spot and didn't know why it popped into his head. But it was a piece of dialogue that stuck with him. When Cameron won the best director Academy Award, he famously yelled out, "I'm the king of the world" before walking off the stage with his statuette. He was criticized by some for the seemingly grandiose reference, but Cameron would say later he was misconstrued.

"I took a lot of flak for the line, but I think the fans understood I was trying to express my joy at the moment," he said. "If you think about what Jack is saying here, 'I don't have a dime in my pocket but it doesn't matter, I'm happy right now in this moment' and that's what I was trying to express at the Academy Awards, not some sense of triumph."

In terms of the public's embrace of the scene and the statement, that developed instantly. In 1998 the Passenger Vessel Association sent its members a "Titanic Alert." It warned crews to be aware of potential copy-cats and said they might consider closing or roping "off the extreme bow access area of [their] vessel."

For those seeking a piece of the scene, it doesn't come cheap. The jacket DiCaprio wore when he uttered these words went up for auction in 2014 with a guide price of $50,000 to $70,000. ★

Hollywood ending

Anybody working in Hollywood can tell you the town isn't a place full of too many happy endings.

To wit, studio mogul Jack Warner, actor-producer Douglas Fairbanks, and theater impresario Sid Grauman once sat down to dinner at the famed Brown Derby Restaurant. Fairbanks complained that the table was uneven, to which part-owner Wilson Mizner supposedly retorted, "How can you expect anything in Hollywood to be on the level?"

Errol Flynn said it was a place "where they have great respect for the dead but none for the living." While Gregory Peck observed, Hollywood was "where you often find a combination of hot heads and cold shoulders."

But for all the criticism for the town, the formula for happy endings, known globally as *Hollywood endings*, is one that dates back to the start of film. Life may not always turn out well, but when the lights dimmed at the movies, patrons could be assured that they could live the dream.

In the 1930s veteran actor-producer-director Wesley Ruggles ruminated on why Hollywood relied on tying up films with pretty bows. In part, he thought it went back to the industry's primordial days when scripts were often done on the fly. Dubbing movie endings "the Keystone finish" after the early comedy studio run by Mack Sennett (see *Keystone Cops*, p. 96), Ruggles said it was just easier to make things work out when you didn't have a lot of time to ruminate over options.

"Anywhere you turn you run into the Keystone finish, and the most one can say for it is that it proves God's in his Hollywood heaven," the *New York Times* wrote in 1936. "Cities may crumble, plague may strike and zombies run amok, but only the villain (the unwanted husband, the unwelcome suitor or the tax collector) is in jeopardy."

While Ruggles had his term, using the *Hollywood ending* descriptor dates to at least the 1920s. By the 1940s the expression had bled into the real world. A dramatic 1944 victory by a local baseball team in the East Liverpool, Ohio, area was described as a "Hollywood ending." Since then the expression has grown steadily as a catchphrase for great finishes or for those moments when people are trying to sell you on a dream. In 1984 a reporter criticized President Ronald Reagan for offering an unrealized "Hollywood ending" to his plan to reduce federal spending for the needy, followed by the private sector picking up the slack.

For those who turn a jaundiced eye to the film industry, take heart that calling someone *Hollywood* as a criticism has picked up steam. While it's used as an adjective to reflect a person or activity being glamorous or dramatic dates back to the 1920s, its application to reflect a shallow and flashy individual has become quite popular over the past handful of decades.

In sync

Oh, Justin Timberlake, Lance Bass, and the other members of that seminal boy band *NSYNC, if only you knew the amount of sweat and toil that was required by the film community to truly fulfill the group's name—or at least the less pop-*eriffic* version of it: *in sync.*

At first this idea of combining images and sound was a pretty humble one. For early silent pictures, the goal was to have a pianist playing the appropriate music live at the cinema at just the right time. One of the problems here was that audiences often tired of what was deemed the perfectly synchronized melody for a scene. For example, Gioachino Rossini's *William Tell Overture* became so common during chases that audiences would groan at its sound.

This issue would be taken care of by the use of original music, which was being produced by 1915. Still, the desire for the quality control that technology could provide drove scientists. (After all, a bad pianist could ruin the mood even with a good score.) *In sync* was an abbreviation for *in synchrony*—or, later, *in synchronization*—and was

Continued on p. 90

> ## "It's alive, it's alive!"
> ## —Henry Frankenstein (Colin Clive),
> ## *Frankenstein* (1931)

This line—and the one that followed it in the original screenplay—created more than a dramatic moment: It raised an existential question.

Upon animating his creation for the first time, Dr. Frankenstein followed his exclamations about it being alive with "in the name of God, now I know what it's like to be a god."

Such a statement didn't sit well with everyone. Local censors in a handful of states, from Kansas to Massachusetts, called for numerous changes to the movie, including excising the mention of God in the famous "it's alive" moment. These state boards believed it was blasphemy and Universal Pictures acquiesced, dubbing in thunderous claps over the divine comments in those regions. During a later rerelease, the industry's own censor, the Hays Office, required the line be cut in all prints of the film.

Even with those questions of the morality in this adaptation of Mary Shelley's classic novel, screenwriters Garrett Fort and Francis Edwards Faragoh were lauded for their work.

"The adaptation to the screen of such a story was obviously a task of extreme difficulty, and it speaks volumes for the ability of Garrett Fort and Francis Edwards Faragoh that they were able to turn out such a finished piece of work as is this screenplay," the *Hollywood Reporter* wrote in its 1931 review.

While Faragoh, who received an Oscar nomination for another 1931 film, *Little Caesar*, would leave the genre, Fort became well known for his writing in the science-fiction/fantasy space between his efforts on *Frankenstein* and the screenplays for *Dracula* (1931) and *Dracula's Daughter* (1936).

Despite Fort's success, the deeper meaning of "it's alive" (not to mention the menacing bloodsucking of Dracula) did not sit well with the writer. A syndicated 1937 article claimed that Fort had difficulty sleeping because "The wrath of Dracula invaded his dreams. Frankenstein's monster tormentingly mastered his reveries."

To combat it, he began following a spiritualist named Meher Baba in an effort to fully understand the meaning of life. He became so committed he moved to India. Ultimately, Fort would grow disillusioned and eventually return to Hollywood. Sadly, he never fully recovered, dying of an overdose of sleeping pills in 1945 at the age of forty-five. ★

used to describe getting the pictures up on the screen aligned with a phonograph playing the sound.

"The talking picture is no more than a sketch or play reproduced by means of motion pictures and the phonograph working in synchrony, that is, the phonograph says 'Curse you, Jack Dalton' at the same moment that the pictures show the player enunciating these words," a 1913 book called *The Technique of the Photoplay* explained.

But even when technicians thought they cracked this element, there was still a problem. Celluloid film could easily burn, requiring individual frames that were damaged to be cut off. Many times those edits wouldn't impact the viewing experience as the respliced film could still appear smooth to the eye. However, when trying to align sound with the newly condensed picture, it was a disaster.

"Synchrony between film and disk could be attainted," a 1918 book called *How Motion Pictures Are Made* said, "but prevention of the film breaking was impossible. When the film was rejoined several frames were missing . . . which naturally made the balance between sight and audition correspondingly difficult to attain."

The answer came in the form of combining the picture and the sound into one package by placing a sound strip directly on the film. Numerous masterminds worked on this process for decades, with Lee de Forest being the first to make a high-profile showing of its magic in 1924. Three years later *The Jazz Singer* debuted as the inaugural full-length talking picture.

The strip on the film containing the words, music, and sound effects would be called the *soundtrack*. This gave us the starting point for that useful idiom when you're exasperated as a parent because your kids are arguing and you sigh, "That's the soundtrack of my life." When we talk about being *in sync* or *out of sync* with friends, family, or colleagues, those expressions were mid-twentieth century innovations, while the band *NSYNC was a 1995 creation.

In the limelight

The man who came up with the idea of the limelight never seemed too bothered that he was never *in the limelight* for the invention. With a name worthy of his brilliantly glaring invention, Sir Goldsworthy Gurney was certainly a talented inventor. In the early 1820s he figured out that using a blow pipe to apply an oxygen-hydrogen mix to a small ball of lime could create the most glorious flame. One 1901 encyclopedia said that it could shine bright for up to 112 miles.

An early fan of the creation was the prominent surveyor Captain Thomas Drummond, who was a member of the British Royal Engineers and relied on the powerful torch to help him map the coast of west Scotland in the mid-1820s. While the good captain didn't appear to ever take credit for the invention, his fame led to the light becoming known as the Drummond Light.

With the limelight's ability to offer an intense and fixed beam, London theater owners co-opted it for the stage in 1837. In June of that year, the salesmanship spirit of the theater was on full display when Frederick Gye, who used the limelight at his establishment called the Rotunda, dubbed the dazzling addition *Phoshelioulamproteron*. The new torch certainly got attention. As the British film critic Percy Fitzgerald said, the limelight "really threw open the realms of glittering fairyland."

While Gurney didn't fight to obtain attention for his limelight, he did want credit for another innovation. It was called the steam blast pipe, which was a handy device that increased the speed of locomotives. So bothered by Gurney's lack of recognition on this matter, the inventor's daughter, Anna, wrote the *Times* of London in 1876, imploring the august newspaper to set the record straight.

For what it's worth, Gurney may have been wise not to take too much credit for the limelight. The device was great at brightening an actor onstage, but it was also a major fire hazard. As author Bill Bryson points out in his 2010 book *At Home*, one 1889 study said nearly 10,000 people died in British theater fires during that century. No doubt, the light often attributed to Drummond led to many of those tragedies.

In the early 1900s the limelight was replaced by safer electric options. But the linguistic imprint of the white-hot theater light had already been secured. It was used metaphorically by the 1870s to represent having all the attention pointed your way. (*Geek note*: The alternative *in the spotlight* also emerged during this period.)

In particular, it's often associated with so many politicians' insatiable look-at-me approach. As future US President Calvin Coolidge put it in his 1919 collection of speeches and messages, *Have Faith in Massachusetts*: "We need more of the Office Desk and less of the Show Window in politics. Let men in office substitute the midnight oil for the limelight."

It's showtime!

Very few words, if any, reflect the entertainment industry more than *show*. I mean, we don't call it the *acting business*, we call it *show business*. Nevertheless, the term originally had nothing to do with theatrical performance.

Show came into the English language through the German (*scou*) and the Dutch (*schowwe*) and was basically used to mean inspecting or looking at something. With that context, it makes sense that its first application was primarily by military men. *To make a show* was in use by the 1500s for a demonstration of military strength. In the late 1700s it was inching its way into theater, but a *show* was judged something different—a more ostentatious activity—than a proper dramatic display.

The Irish statesman Edmund Burke made this distinction in a 1797 letter complaining about the over-the-top productions in London at the time. "The dresses, the scenes, the decorations of every kind, I am told are in a new style of splendor and magnificence; whether to

Continued on p. 94

Lights! Camera! Takeoff?
Movie Glitz at Airports

At some point a Hollywood talent agent has surely been asked the following question by a star client who has everything: "How do I get an airport named after me?" Let's just say, it doesn't come easy.

In 1941 the great comedian Will Rogers received the distinction in Oklahoma City—but only after he died in a 1935 plane crash. (*Geek note*: Rogers, an Oklahoma native, was an avid flyer, and the aviation community was keen to honor him. Chicago almost named an airport after him in 1935, and the tiny town of Barrow, Alaska, near where he went down, did change the title of its airport to memorialize Rogers and his pilot, Wiley Post.)

Decades later, in 1979, a California assemblyman wanted to rename Los Angeles International Airport after John Wayne but was met with tremendous resistance. "I think it's ridiculous," said then-assemblywoman and future US congresswoman Maxine Waters. "I want it named Farrah Fawcett-Majors Airport." After all the pushback, the Duke had to settle for top-lining an airport south of L.A., in Orange County.

Still, Wayne's triumph definitely caught Bob Hope's attention. The comedian would say to his family at the time, "Wouldn't it be nice to have an airport named after me someday?" His daughter Linda Hope added with a chuckle years later that "he was always a little jealous of John Wayne." In 2003 Hope got his wish in Burbank, California . . . months after he had died. Then, in a tragic postscript, local officials voted in May 2016 to rebrand the location as Hollywood Burbank Airport, though they promised Bob Hope Airport would remain its "legal name."

As for longtime B-actor Ronald Reagan, he wouldn't have gotten his name on an airport based on his acting career alone (no offense to his workmanlike performance in *Bedtime for Bonzo*). But the two-term president got on the marquee at Washington, D.C.'s most central airport in 1998.

The following are the select few film power players who have claimed this unique achievement.

- Bob Hope Airport, Burbank, California
- Federico Fellini Airport, Rimini, Italy
- Indiana County Jimmy Stewart Airport, Indiana, Pennsylvania
- John Wayne Airport, Santa Ana, California
- Ronald Reagan Washington National Airport, Arlington, Virginia
- Wiley Post-Will Rogers (Post/Rogers) Memorial Airport, Barrow, Alaska
- Will Rogers World Airport, Oklahoma City, Oklahoma

the advantage of our dramatick taste, upon whole, I very much doubt," he wrote. "It is a sh[o]w and a spectacle, not a play, that is exhibited."

Burke's tastes aside, the stage world—along with circuses (see "A Jumbo Entertainer: P. T. Barnum," p. 151) and other forms of entertainment—fully embraced *show* in the 1800s, and the word quickly became a fountainhead for idioms and expressions. *The show must go on* was among the first to emerge. An early figurative print example can be found in an 1870 edition of the *Fort Wayne Daily Democrat* (Indiana). After reporting about political problems amongst Republican candidates for an upcoming election, the paper declared it was "truly a sad state of affairs. We sympathize deeply. But the show must go on." The ease in which this reference was used indicates the phrase was already well established in the performance space.

Showtime, to simply indicate when a play would begin, can be regularly found at the start of the 1900s, and the expression *it's showtime* as a broader way to indicate that some worthwhile action was about to take place was being applied beyond the entertainment world by 1926. That year, a *Life* magazine ad for the wheel company Budd-Michelin touted its new line with the opening phrase "It's Show-time again."

In the 1920s other firmly established phrases included *stealing the show* for someone who grabs all the attention in a production, and a *show-stopper* for an actor whose talent was so great the applause halted the routine. *Get the show on the road*, which likely got its inspiration from traveling circuses, appears to have developed a little later (also see *showboat*, p. 149).

Jump the shark

Fonzie looked so cool in that leather jacket, but even he eventually had a defining moment of ignominy. It came while trying to water-ski (in the jacket no less!) over a shark. For those confused millennials, this is a reference to the longtime TV hit *Happy Days* and how it inspired *jump the shark* as an expression for that tipping point when something free-falls in quality.

The phrase was coined on the campus of the University of Michigan in 1987. A guy named John Hein and his buddies were chatting about that precise instance when a TV show journeys from good to awful. Everyone gave suggestions, including a guy named Sean Connolly, who offered up Fonzie jumping the shark. His suggestion stuck, and when Hein started a website to discuss the "defining moment when you know from now on . . . it's all downhill . . . it will never be the same" for a TV program, he named it after Connolly's exemplar candidate. Hein launched www.JumpTheShark.com in 1997 and it became a wild hit. So much so, that in 2006, he sold the company to *TV Guide* owner Gemstar for a reported seven-figure sum.

But was jumping the shark really the moment when *Happy Days jumped the shark*?

In 2010 the writer of that fateful moment offered a vigorous defense.

Fred Fox Jr. pointed out that when that episode aired on September 20, 1977, it was a huge hit, placing third in the weekly TV ratings with more than thirty million viewers.

"All successful shows eventually start to decline, but this was not *Happy Days'* time," he wrote in the pages of the *Los Angeles Times*. "Consider: It was the 91st episode and the fifth season. If this was really the beginning of a downward spiral, why did the show stay on the air for six more seasons and shoot an additional 164 episodes? Why did we rank among the Top 25 in five of those six seasons?"

At first, Fox was stung by his work serving as a code phrase for a turn toward failure, but over time he became Zen about the connection.

"I likened the popularity [of the expression] to a new fad, where someone jumps on the proverbial bandwagon and soon everyone is doing it, for no rhyme or reason, like the riding the mechanical bull craze," he said. "It was ludicrous. All I could do was laugh."

One thing is for certain: This craze has definitely outlasted the life span of mechanical bulls. The expression has been included in the *Oxford English Dictionary* and, at various points in time, pundits have asked whether everyone and everything from President Barack Obama to the sport of Formula One racing has *jumped the shark*.

Keystone Cops

We may have never had the bumbling *Keystone Cops* (also known as the *Keystone Kops*) if not for a gambling debt. The great slapstick comedy producer Mack Sennett suggested forming the Keystone Film Company to onetime bookmakers Adam Kessel and Charles O. Baumann as part of "a quick-thinking sales pitch . . . during a rather forceful collection attempt on a gambling debt he owed," according to Sennett biographer Brent E. Walker.

Sennett's fledgling company started making silent films in 1912, and within the first year of business, these policemen, who couldn't seem to get anything right, became central characters. They'd go on wild chases, run into walls, and consistently make fools of themselves for the amusement of the audience. Named after the studio, this slapstick ensemble was a huge hit. (*Geek note*: Sennett said the Keystone name came from a Pennsylvania train he saw passing by one day; "if it was good enough for the railroad, it was good enough for us," he said.)

Walker suggests that Sennett's blundering troupe was so deeply embraced by moviegoers because the savvy producer picked just the right people to lampoon.

"Sennett . . . realized that even though politicians, monarchs and influential captains of industry were the world's most powerful authority figures, the average laborer of the period never encountered these types of men in their entire lives," he wrote. "In their communities, the cop on the beat was the flesh-and-blood representative of his higher authority, and to take him down a peg was a sure laughter tonic for the working class."

To be sure, the cultural impact of the *Keystone Cops* was nearly instantaneous. By 1915 newspapers were already calling them "famous," and within the same decade, real-life cops who made mistakes were slapped with the *Keystone Cop* moniker. From there, it became an off-handed expression for all sorts of actions that, as the *Oxford English Dictionary* puts it, are "shambolic or farcical."

Those who have been likened to *Keystone Cops* over the years have truly varied, including chess players, replacement baseball umpires, Kenyan authorities, and dancers at the School of American Ballet.

While Sennett gave the American lexicon this expression, he would look back nearly fifty years after the founding of the Keystone

Continued on p. 100

> ## "May the force be with you."
> ## —Han Solo (Harrison Ford) and
> ## General Jan Dodonna (Alex McCrindle),
> ## *Star Wars: Episode IV—A New Hope* (1977)

A long time ago in a story far, far before *Star Wars*, the force existed.

The franchise's creator, George Lucas, first used the concept in his debut film *THX 1138*. In that movie, which was completed in 1971, one of the characters discusses that world's state-sanctioned deity, saying "there must be something independent; a force, reality." In 2005 Lucas told *Wired* magazine that his use in *THX 1138* and, subsequently, in the *Star Wars* films was "an echo" of a phrase used in a 1963 experimental film by Canadian filmmaker Arthur Lipsett called *21-87*.

Lucas further elaborated on the philosophy behind the term in the definitive book, *The Making of Star Wars*.

"The 'Force of others' is what all basic religions are based on, especially the eastern religions, which is, essentially, that there is a force, God, whatever you want to call it," he said.

By the time the original *Star Wars* movie reached theaters, the philosophy was fleshed out a bit. As Obi-Wan Kenobi (played by Alec Guinness) explained: "The Force is what gives a Jedi his power. It's an energy field created by all living things. It surrounds us and penetrates us. It binds the galaxy together."

In addition, the phraseology for wishing somebody the support of the Force was also modified. In Lucas's first rough draft in 1974, his characters say on more than one occasion, "May the force of others be with you."

While the "others" was scrapped along the way, the structure of "may the" did remain. Laurent Bouzereau, who wrote *Star Wars: The Annotated Screenplays*, points out that this might have been a subtle nod to the Christian phraseology of "May the Lord be with you in your spirit," which was often used as a sign-off by St. Paul in his letters.

The final wording proved particularly handy in the era of viral social media. Playing off the phrase, #maythefourthbewithyou has become a commonly hashtagged rallying cry from *Star Wars* fans on May 4. Lucasfilm has even adopted it as the official Star Wars Day. And while this play off "may the force be with you" seems like a recent creation, it may have actually been coined just two years after *Star Wars* came out . . . by supporters of Margaret Thatcher.

After Thatcher won election as Britain's first female prime minister, her Conservative Party took out a half-page ad in London's *Evening News* on May 4, 1979, according to Alan Arnold, who wrote on the making of *The Empire Strikes Back* for Lucasfilm.

"The message [in the newspaper], referring to the day of victory, was 'May the Fourth Be With You, Maggie. Congratulations,'" Arnold wrote, according to StarWars.com. "[It was] further proof of the extent to which *Star Wars* has influenced us all." ★

Film Company and wonder to what extent words got in the way of comedy. In 1959 the producer lamented that film humor wasn't what it was in the days of his *Keystone Cops*.

"Maybe people are paying too much attention to grammar today," he said. "I don't think there's too many belly laughs in grammar."

Lay an egg

The venerable entertainment industry trade publication *Variety* has long been known for dropping its own version of showbiz slang into its copy. The most famous example is probably the 1935 statement "Stix Nix Hick Pix" (translation: Rural Midwesterners weren't interested in films set on the farm).

But when it comes to using Hollywood lingo to offer a bit of gallows humor, *Variety*'s notable moment came when it ran a banner headline the day after the stock market crashed in 1929. *Variety* caustically exclaimed on October 30: "Wall St. Lays an Egg."

If you take a moment to ponder it, this is quite an odd expression. What's so bad about laying an egg? Surely a little poultry productivity isn't a bad thing?

The most popular answer to explain how the phrase found its way to being a statement for full-blown failure—whether on the screen or in the boardroom—is it came from the sport of baseball via cricket.

Beginning in the nineteenth century, when a cricket batter failed to score, it was said to be a *duck* or a *duck egg* (as the oval shape looked like a zero). Baseball picked that imagery up at the start of the 1900s but shifted it to a *goose egg*. From there, members of both the baseball world and the stage supposedly embraced the broader egg-laying metaphor.

Still, it's unclear who used it first. *Variety* had the term in print by 1926 when it panned a New York burlesque show, saying it had "laid enough eggs to feed the starving Armenians." Three years later a journalist invoked it when discussing concerns about baseball's New York Giants' lack of a good second baseman.

The reporter wrote: "in the inelegant phraseology of the curbstone, [Giants' manager] John McGraw must be getting ready to lay an egg . . . this season." Clearly, in New York at least, both groups employed the expression in the second half of the 1920s. But it's generally faded on the baseball diamond while Hollywood's long-term fascination with the expression likely helped spur and maintain its general usage.

Incidentally, the phrase *laying an egg* was actually used for a different purpose before ballplayers and stage regulars got a hold of it. World War I pilots would describe bombs as "eggs" and would say they were *laying an egg* when dropping them. For those of you who might think this was the start of the phrase—after all, *a bomb* often represents failure in America (e.g., "I really *bombed* that test")—you should reconsider. Using a *bomb* to signal a bad performance appears to be a mid-twentieth century creation, and the humiliation of *laying an egg*, in a figurative sense, was in place well before.

Leading role

Acting is not supposed to be a competitive sport. And while anyone who has clawed their way to jobs in Hollywood or embarked on an Academy Award marketing campaign might argue otherwise, at the least, industry folk try not to bring attention to its dog-eat-dog nature.

Considering that fact, using the word *leading*, which more often than not we now use in an athletic sense, seems to break that silent code: There can be no doubt, the man or woman with the *leading role* is certainly in first place in a production.

Of course, that wasn't the intended meaning when it first appeared in the 1600s. The purpose of *leading* at the time was to primarily describe, well, a leader or a person who was the most prominent figure in an endeavor.

Continued on p. 104

> "My momma always said, 'Life was like a box of chocolates. You never know what you're gonna get.'"
> —Forrest Gump (Tom Hanks),
> *Forrest Gump* (1994)

Big-screen adaptations of literature often lead to snobby literati scoffing, "the book was so much better than the film."

For many, *Forrest Gump* is an exception to that rule.

Author Winston Groom received mainly mixed reviews for *Forrest Gump*'s printed source material. As *Publishers Weekly* put it: "Groom, author of *Better Times Than These*, has written better books than this." In contrast, the movie won the 1995 Academy Award for best picture.

While admittedly there are some detractors of the film who suggest it's overly sentimental, so much of the movie's success came down to how the filmmakers reimagined the project. In the book Gump was a 6-foot-6, 242-pound hulk; in the movie he was a nimble, fast-moving man. In the book he saved Mao Zedong from drowning and traveled to space as an astronaut. The movie streamlines and modifies Gump's adventures.

Equally noticeable were the language changes writer Eric Roth infused into the screenplay. Winning lines like "Run, Forrest run" and "Stupid is as stupid does" weren't in the book. Instead, adding phrases that were unique to Gump was part of Roth's scriptwriting blueprint.

"I tried to create aphorisms that didn't particularly make sense, but they seemed to make sense within the context of this character," Roth told the *Los Angeles Times* in 2010. "My own mother used to say, 'Handsome is as handsome does.' I had Forrest say, 'Stupid is as stupid does.'"

In the case of likening life to a box of chocolates, Roth, who won the adapted screenplay Oscar for *Gump* in 1995, actually had inspiration from the book.

Groom's first line in the print version was: "Let me say this: bein a idiot is no box of chocolates. People laugh, lose patience, treat you shabby."

Initially, Roth's plan was to simply have Gump say, "Life is like a box of chocolates." But the film's director, Robert Zemeckis, balked.

"Upon going through the script, Bob demanded, 'What the hell does this mean?'" Roth said. At that point the screenwriter explained, "You know, you never know what you're going to get." The explanation worked for Zemeckis and that portion of the line was added.

While Groom's prose was changed, the author generally didn't mind—although he noted that the movie version "took the rough edges off the character." Groom had also always pictured beefy actor John Goodman in the role of Gump. Then again, how could he have been too bothered? Before the film came out, the book sold about 30,000 units. Within a couple of month of the movie's release, there were approximately 1.4 million copies in circulation. ★

Though not as common nowadays as using it in conjunction with the status of a baseball game (e.g., the Red Sox are *leading* the Yankees going into the ninth inning), this form still comes up somewhat regularly (think, "leading scientists believe the earth is round").

What makes *leading role* a term with specific theater roots is the inclusion of the word *role*. That word comes directly from the French *rôle*, which was used in the 1500s as we use it today—a "character represented by an actor," according to the *Oxford English Dictionary*.

Martin Harrison, who wrote *The Language of Theater*, believes that combining *leading* and *role* to represent the star of a show was inspired by the military. "The term is usually employed only for experienced actors," he wrote, "and seems to come from a military metaphor—*leading one's company* (as into battle)." Alternatively, the *New York Times's* longtime "On Language" columnist, William Safire, posited that it came from the sea and "navigation's leading light or guiding light."

Whichever is correct, the phrase *leading role*—as well as *leading lady* and *leading man*—were all popular descriptors for theater stars by the second half of the 1800s. From there those expressions, along with a *starring role*—became idioms for being the key figure in all walks of life. Extending the metaphor, phrases like *supporting role* and *bit part* (see p. 15) also crossed over into everyday lexicon.

Looney Tunes

If *Looney Tunes* had been devised in today's litigious society, the term might not have lasted long enough to spawn a great idiom for a crazy person or situation. The series of movie cartoons that would eventually become TV staples were created in 1930 by animators Hugh Harman and Rudolf Ising.

The pair were among the first animators Walt Disney had hired back in Kansas City when he started his animating efforts. But Harman and Ising parted ways with Disney and were hired on by Warner

Bros. to emulate the success their old studio was having with short cartoons set to music under the banner "Silly Symphonies."

In embarking on this project, the animators not only followed Disney's thematic trail, they also poked at the name the Mouse House was using. *Looney Tunes* was a parody of that Silly Symphonies moniker. In fact, Harman and Ising would soon double down on the derivative riff by starting a second brand of animated shorts called "Merrie Melodies."

Despite executing a maneuver that nowadays would likely get a posse of lawyers itching to break down *Looney Tunes'* door with a satchel full of cease-and-desist orders, it doesn't appear Disney ever acted on the title resemblances. In fact, in 1937 when Harman and Ising were in some financial trouble, Disney gave them some work on the "Silly Symphonies."

"If Walt ever said anything about that, disdainful or otherwise, in any interviews or interoffice correspondence, I've never run across it—and I've seen a lot of interviews and correspondence," animation and Walt Disney expert J. B. Kaufman said. "He and Harman and Ising certainly had their differences, but at heart I don't think Walt was a vindictive guy."

When it comes to the name's broader implications, the connection between the *Looney Tunes* title and what it could represent off-screen was made very early. "A group of serious men meet to hold a story conference before a new 'Looney Tunes' is begun," a 1931 *Washington Post* article said. "Then suddenly—the logical plot once constructed—they take leave of all sanity and become like a group of demented men as they put the 'looney' into the 'Looney Tunes.'"

Still, despite that reference, *Looney Tunes*, or as it's sometimes written *loony tunes*, didn't gain a toehold as an idiom until the 1980s. In 1985 President Ronald Reagan gave it a push when he criticized nations he believed were breaking international law. "We are especially not

Continued on p. 108

> "Roads? Where we're going,
> we don't need roads."
> —Dr. Emmett Brown (Christopher
> Lloyd), *Back to the Future* (1985)

Ronald Reagan, who had a penchant for movie quotes (see *Go ahead, make my day*, p. 22, and *Looney Tunes*, p. 104), boosted this line's big-screen afterlife when he referenced it in his 1986 State of the Union address.

"Never has there been a more exciting time to be alive, a time of rousing wonder and heroic achievement," he said. "As they said in the film *Back to the Future*, 'Where we're going, we don't need roads.'"

Little did the president know that he almost didn't have that piece of dialogue to punctuate his upbeat message. When the film's actors convened to shoot the final scene of the movie, the script initially had the line ". . . your kids Marty, something's got to be done about your kids" as the comedy's closing statement before the characters loaded into the DeLorean and took to the air, blasting into the future. But as they were setting up, the movie's brain trust, which included director-writer Robert Zemeckis, writer-producer Bob Gale, and actors Christopher Lloyd and Michael J. Fox, sensed it wasn't quite right.

"It was one of those moments when Bob Zemeckis or the actors said something," Gale said. "We need to have a breath here."

Logistically, they realized that an additional shot was required inside the car before the time-traveling vehicle could fly. Back in the mid-1980s, filmmakers didn't have the visual-effects technology to believably show a real car pulling out of a driveway and then seamlessly taking off into the sky. Instead, an in-between moment featuring the actors talking in the DeLorean before a cutaway to a miniature of the car jettisoning into the air was necessary to smooth the transition.

Gale can't remember how the added dialogue was devised but recalls it was done on the set. He is also certain that "it was purely coincidence" that the phrase echoes a popular rewording of another great movie quote: "Badges? We don't need no stinking badges." (*Geek note:* Those words were never actually uttered in the 1948 film *The Treasure of the Sierra Madre*; the actual lines were, "Badges? We ain't got no badges. We don't need no badges. I don't have to show you any stinking badges.")

However it was chosen, everyone must have liked it because no alternatives were filmed or, it appears, even seriously contemplated. Still, Lloyd probably played with the words, giving the filmmakers options.

"We always shot more than one take," Gale said. "The interesting thing about Christopher Lloyd is he rarely did it the same way twice. But every way he did it, it was good. He'd mix up his delivery of the line, and it's possible that he may have said it a few different ways."

When Zemeckis and Gale put together the two *Back to the Future* sequels, they definitely harkened back to many elements in the original film. The two would joke that audiences "want to see the same movie but different." Nevertheless, giving this memorable statement an encore was never discussed.

"This was a case where the line is a setup for a wonderful payoff—that the car flies," Gale said. "You can't do that a second time. The only way you could have done that was if the car turned into a submarine." ★

going to tolerate these attacks from outlaw states run by the strangest collection of misfits, 'Looney Tunes,' and squalid criminals since the advent of the Third Reich," he said. At the same time, the phrase was developing a use in law enforcement circles for a crazy person. This also gave the expression a bounce in the general lexicon.

While *Looney Tunes* took some time to catch on, two other catch-phrases from the cartoons were already in circulation. *That's all folks!* (generally pronounced by Porky Pig as *Th-Th-That's all folks!*) were the ending words for *Looney Tunes* cartoons from 1930. Bugs Bunny's famous greeting *What's up, Doc?* emerged in 1940. Both were parroted by everyday people long before the 1980s.

Marquee

The dream of every wannabe star seeing their name in lights up on a theater's *marquee* is so common it's become trope. However, if you went back a couple of centuries ago and delivered that cliché, you'd likely get a lot of quizzical looks.

The idea of a *marquee* likely came via the French royal title *marquis*. A marquis (or as it's written in English, *marquess*)—which in British hierarchy was below a duke but above an earl—was a person of much power. Back in the day, when war came, that person was expected to round up his followers and fight on behalf of the king or queen. On the battlefield, the marquess would get a special, spacious tent, which was colloquially called the *marquee*.

Over time *marquee* became synonymous with a type of big tent used for all sorts of major occasions. For example in 1888, the *New York Times* wrote that the New York Horticultural Society held its annual exhibition "in a marquee erected especially for the purpose." Among those who used this term were circuses and traveling shows. For instance, the famed entertainer Buffalo Bill was in London in 1887 and held a breakfast in honor of former US Senator Simon Cameron "in the marquee of the Wild West camp," the *Washington Post* reported.

From there, the word started to develop an additional meaning. For the performers who used these *marquees*, they'd begin to list their acts on the front canvass flap of the tent. By the 1900s this signage was being called a *marquee*, probably first on a tent and then on a building. In 1911 Baltimore's *Sun* told how Ford's Opera House in the city had gone through renovations that included "an elaborate marquee of steel and bronze."

Fancy *marquees*, like the one erected at Ford's Opera House, prompted the word's metaphorical use for a top-notch attraction in a theater or otherwise. *Marquee value*, as a Hollywood expression to reflect bankable stars, was in use by the 1930s. Today, marquee value can be brought from all types, like hotshot venture capitalists or established politicians stumping for other candidates.

More recently sportswriters have been drawn to the idea of a *marquee matchup*. That's when two teams—or sometimes two boxers—of big-time prominence square off. A *marquee win* is also popular with sports scribes when talking about an especially valuable victory against a good opponent.

Then there's the computer term *marquee tag*, which is used in HTML to create a type of scrolling text on the side of the screen. Considering how annoying that can be, it's not a *marquee* most like seeing.

Melodramatic

The next time someone in your family gets *melodramatic* ("OMG, I'll simply die if I have to wear that outfit to school!"), tell them that they're not allowed to be extravagantly sensational without some good music to accompany their rant.

You see, the origins of the *melodrama* required some pleasing tunes. The word comes from the seventeenth-century Italian *melodramma*, which was typically used to describe a type of opera. All sorts of European countries liked the term and created their own versions. For example, the French had *mélodrame*, the Germans often went with *melodram*, and the English opted for *melodrama* or *melodrame*. In each case, early productions bearing this name featured talking over music. What is less clear is how the word went from essentially representing an opera to our current understanding, which is an incident-filled drama, usually heavy on romance, heroes, and villains.

Here's what's known: Melodrama entered English in the 1700s and seems to have made its transformation away from operatic work before the end of that century. Furthermore, regardless of what led to the change in meaning, we can be sure that in the first two decades of the 1800s, this new version of drama became the rage. It was so big that a British dramatist and theatrical promoter named Thomas John Dibdin, seemingly looking to capitalize on the interest, named an 1818 production "Melodrame Mad!"

If you're among the many who rolls their eyes at any sort of *melodrama* in your life, you'd be in good company as some of the critics in this British Regency era were also not fans of this popular overblown style.

"The taste then, for melo-drama, must arise from an inertness in the minds of the spectators, and a wish to be amused without the slightest exertion on their own parts, or an exercise whatever in their intellectual powers," a reviewer wrote in 1818.

Despite critiques like that, there is an argument that melodrama became more than a form of theater during this period—it became a state of mind. In her 1995 book *Melodramatic Tactics: Theatricalized Dissent in the English Marketplace, 1800–1885*, an academic named Elaine Hadley claimed that this stage style reflected itself in many of the actions of British society during this period in what she called the "melodramatic mode."

Beyond those social ramifications, everyday speech was certainly captivated by the concept. Figuratively, *melodrama* and the adjective *melodramatic* were often used for nonthespian occasions from the start of the 1800s.

Continued on p. 112

They're *G-r-r-r-eat:*
TV Commercials

Television commercials are an art form all their own. Just ask Jason Bateman. "I've always loved commercials," the comedic actor said in 2010. "I like working out how to organically weave a brand's message into the writing process. It's like an improv show, where comics ask the audience to throw out a word and a skit is built around it."

In all fairness, whatever spontaneity the copywriters come up with is undoubtedly vetted by multiple focus groups before ever hitting our screens at home. Still, whether it's the repetition or the uncanny ability of Madison Avenue marketing gurus to tap into our subconscious, ad phrases and expressions that we hear on TV—and, of course, experience through coordinated print/Internet campaigns—have long trickled into our lexicon to be restated and parodied over and over again. Here's a cross-section of commercial lines that fit that bill:

- "They're *g-r-r-r-eat!*"—Frosted Flakes (cereal), 1952
- "But wait, there's more"—Ron Popeil (various infomercials), 1950s
- "Sometimes you feel like a nut, sometimes you don't"—Almond Joy/Mounds bars (candy), 1953
- "Takes a licking and keeps on ticking"—Timex (watch), 1956
- "Good to the last drop"—Maxwell House (coffee), 1959
- "That's a spicy meatball" and "I can't believe I ate the whole thing"—Alka Seltzer (antacid), 1969
- "Tastes great! Less filling!"—Miller Lite (beer), 1974
- "Reach out and touch someone"—AT&T (phone), 1979
- "Be all that you can be"—US Army (recruitment ad), 1981

- "Time to make the donuts"—Dunkin' Donuts (doughnuts), 1983
- "Where's the beef?"—Wendy's (restaurant) 1984
- "I'm not a doctor, but I play one on TV"—Vicks Formula 44 (cough syrup) 1984
- "They keep going and going and going . . ."—Energizer (batteries), 1989
- "Money, it's gotta be the shoes"—Nike (shoes), 1989
- "I've fallen and I can't get up"—LifeCall (medical alarm and protection) 1989
- "Not going anywhere for a while?"—Snickers (candy), 1995
- "Whassup?"—Budweiser (beer), 1999
- "What's in your wallet?"—Capital One (credit card), 2000
- "What happens here, stays here"—Las Vegas Tourism Board (promotional ad), 2003
- "The world's most interesting man"—Dos Equis (beer) 2006

One additional aside: If you want to impress at cocktail parties with another similar theater term that went idiomatic, there's always *histrionics*. This word was used in the nineteenth century to describe acting. Now it's almost exclusively applied to off-the-stage dramatics, dare I say, *melodramatic* behavior.

Mickey Mouse

Mickey Mouse was a rock star by the 1930s. The cartoon character made his debut in 1928 and in 1935 the *New York Times* said he was "the best-known and most popular international figure of his day. One touch of Mickey makes the whole world grin in a very dark hour."

And yet, at the same time elsewhere, *Mickey Mouse* had become a put-down adjective for something either trite or lacking seriousness and, later, for an absurd or useless activity.

What's up with that?

The answer comes from the jazz community. In a world where improvisation and avant-garde sensibilities were king, *Mickey Mouse* was so corporate and uncool. George T. Simon, who beginning in the 1930s was a jazz critic, author, and sometime drummer, explained that it was common during that time period for any "self-respecting jazz musician . . . [to] sneeringly" refer to bland performances as 'mickey-mouse music.'"

"Where the phrase came from, I don't know," he wrote in his 1968 book *The Big Band*, "except perhaps that the music sounded as manufactured and mechanical as Walt Disney's famous character —and projected just about as much emotional depth!"

This pejorative meaning continued to float around in the ether and was sometimes used in the 1930s to also represent something small (presumably in honor of the mouse's diminutive size). But during World War II and the Korean War, it took on new meaning among sailors, who were quite possibly inspired by the jazz usage.

"Who doesn't know that unnecessary or demeaning regulations are 'Mickey Mouse'?" asked former Admiral Elmo R. Zumwalt Jr. in a 1977 *New York Times* article.

Zumwalt, who began active duty in 1942, offered a series of examples of those moments of naval bureaucracy that earned the *Mickey Mouse* modifier.

"If sailors are ordered to slap paint over rusted decks to make the ship look temporarily good for visiting brass, that's Mickey Mouse," he wrote. "If sailors are ordered to do dirty work, not in dungarees but in blue uniforms, which must then be dry-cleaned at personal expense, that is Mickey Mouse."

Mickey Mouse didn't leave most of these servicemen's vocabulary when they returned to regular life, and the term stuck for absurd civilian rules.

Despite the criticism, there's no doubt Mickey Mouse had the last laugh. Disney is one of the world's most powerful media companies and, as its founder Walt Disney said in 1954, "I only hope that we never lose sight of one thing—that it was all started by a mouse."

Miscast

Show business has had its fair share of *miscasts*. For illustrative purposes, I'm going with Sofia Coppola in *The Godfather, Part III* as an example.

While *miscasting* moments mainly occur thanks to bad judgment, at times they have happened without even trying. The great director King Vidor once recounted a story about a pair of studio drivers in the early days of film who mistakenly dropped off two sets of actors at the wrong locations. Rather than waste money on shifting the casts to their rightful places, the directors simply divvied up the roles between their new rosters of performers and went about shooting.

Using the term *miscast* for having a performer in the wrong role—whether accidental or not—has been around since at least the second half of the nineteenth century. As the *Boston Sunday Globe* put it in an 1888 article contemplating a disappointing production: ". . . people crowd the theatre, not to see Shakespeare, but to see Daly's admirable company of artists miscast, vainly struggling against their own sense of what is fit and proper, but putting money into the coffers all the same."

Despite this thespian usage, the word has a much longer history, with a much different definition. Way back in the 1300s, *miscast* meant directing one's eye malevolently (e.g., "The Pirate miscast at his captives"). By the 1600s it was commonly applied to describe miscalculating or adding numbers up incorrectly and, in that same century, it also could mean mislaying an object.

But it was the acting world that led to people metaphorically applying it to any improperly assigned individual or task. That happened before the end of the nineteenth century. An 1898 book called

Madam of the Ivies offered early evidence. Author Elizabeth Phipps Train took it to describe the main character's excitement at arriving at a new job as a caregiver. "I had heretofore been miscast in the role which had been given to me to play," she wrote.

Mob scene

We all fear a *mob scene*. In the best of times, it's just an uncomfortable crowd, and in the worst, well, it can be downright dangerous. While the phrase is often attributed to violent outbursts like riots, the media can be liberal when defining what constitutes one of these. Everything from the opening of the first Whole Foods in Brooklyn to the birth of Prince William and Kate Middleton's first child, George, have apparently created *mob scenes*.

One would assume that *mob scenes* over bulk granola at the Whole Foods are pretty cordial. But even if that's true, they'd likely seem downright chaotic compared to the finely choreographed action of the original *mob scenes*. Why? Because this term was initially created for heavily directed stage moments and became part of the Hollywood lexicon for a scene featuring a big crowd.

In 1862 Baltimore's *Sun* ran an ad hyping a show at the local Front Street Theatre. In outlining the drama's compelling moments, the notice highlighted a snowstorm, a fire, and "The Great Mob Scene." While that's one of the first-known theatrical American references, the stage expression seems certain to predate it, because while it's generally accepted the phrase was popularized by actors and directors, it had been used for nonthespian moments by the 1820s. It's also worth pointing out that even though the expression *mob scene* may be hard to find in print before then, *mob* as a term for a group featured in a stage scene existed in writing by the start of the 1700s. (Coming from the word *mobile*, a *mob* meant either a rabble or, simply, a bunch of people in common conversation at that time as well.)

Continued on p. 118

"Say hello to my little friend!"
—Tony Montana (Al Pacino), *Scarface* (1983)

Sometimes it's not what you say but how you say it. This quote, which was part of Oliver Stone's *Scarface* screenplay, falls into that category.

What has long stood out about this lasting catchphrase was the way Al Pacino delivered the line about a not-so-little gun. As longtime critic Ken Tucker wrote in his book *Scarface Nation: The Ultimate Gangster Movie and How It Changed America*, the line is "more commonly written as the actor enunciated it, 'Say hello to mah leetle *fren*'!"

Though it was seen as unnecessarily stereotypical to some critics, the exaggerated delivery, you could argue, was in line with the movie's wretched excess approach to the story of a Cuban-immigrant-gone-crazy-drug-dealer. To get the accent just right, Pacino, a legendary method actor, worked hard at it. Not only did he have a voice coach who would school him on Spanish grammar and the finer points of a Cuban accent, but he'd also talk like Tony Montana at all times. He would go to dinner with co-stars and he'd continue speaking with Spanish inflections. During wardrobe fittings he'd talk in character.

Another element that gave this piece of dialogue the over-the-top vibe it needed for immortality was the scope of the scene in which it was delivered. The line comes at the end of the movie when Montana is besieged by a hit squad. In the script, writer Oliver Stone said he'd called for only four or five assassins to stalk him. Instead, director Brian De Palma sent a platoon to take out the drug kingpin.

"It was like thirty or forty gunmen," Stone said. "It changes the nature of the film; it was so outrageous at this point, and Brian just kept going and going, and for some reason it works."

Pacino may have contributed the colorful accent and De Palma may have added the cartoon-like violence that provided the cult-like context for the line's success, but as far as Pacino is concerned, Stone deserves credit for what he once described as a "catchy phrase."

"Oliver Stone wrote that text," he said in a 2010 interview. "So when you say, 'say hello to my little friend,' I think of Oliver."

For Stone's part, he's been perplexed by its enduring popularity.

"You can never tell with these things," the screenwriter said in 2002. "Like in *Scarface*, 'Say hello to my little friend.' Gimme a break! The lines can be silly . . . I wrote a lot of what I thought were great lines in other movies and nobody noticed." ★

Early movie producers recognized the value of masses of humanity on the screen and took the figure of speech from the dawn of film. In 1912 the *Motion Picture News* lauded a film called *A Man's Man* for its use of the device, saying, "The production shows one of the finest managed mob scenes. . . . There are nearly seventy-five people in the mob and they are all good . . . all for a purpose and strengthen the ensemble."

Bulked-up, on-screen crowds became so indispensable (see *Cast of thousands*, p. 31) that some backlash quickly ensued. In 1922 journalist and screenwriter Peter Milne criticized the *mob scene* in his book *Motion Picture Directing: The Facts and Theories of the Newest Art.*

"Mob scene follows mob scene, until each scene has no particular meaning, the mass effects grow tiresome and the spectator longs for a glimpse of the story forgotten so long ago by the director," he wrote.

Sadly, it doesn't seem too many people in Hollywood listened to Milne, as some would say filmmakers continue to fall into this trap even today.

Money shot

Bobby Jones was many things: one of the greatest golfers of all time, a beacon of sportsmanship, and a pretty good lawyer. But if he were alive today and were familiar with the common vernacular, the morally upstanding gentleman would probably wince at the knowledge he was also an early practitioner of the *money shot*.

Now, most of us know the money shot as being something not for family viewing. In 1972 the film *Deep Throat* was released. It was the first hard-core pornographic feature-length film and, according to University of California–Berkley academic Linda Williams, one way it distinguished itself from past skin flicks was with the *money shot*. While plotless stag films had all sorts of sex acts going on, a full-length (so to speak) X-rated film needed elements to indicate a scene was ending. Well, showing a dude climaxing to serve as that necessary climax was the answer.

It didn't take long for the term to enjoy elevated status in the porn business. In Stephen Ziplow's 1977 book *The Film Maker's Guide to Pornography*, he explains "'the money shot' is the most important element in the movie and that everything else (if necessary) should be sacrificed at its expense." He added that if you don't have the money shot, "you don't have a porno picture."

Academics have pondered why that release was so important. (The aforementioned Williams offered an interesting theory that it was the embodiment of advanced capitalism.) But whatever its prominent value, the bigger question is: What did it have to do with such a clean-cut figure as Bobby Jones?

According to the *Oxford English Dictionary*, Jones was the earliest-known person to get nervous about delivering a money shot. "Bobby Jones," wrote the *Dunkirk Evening Observer* (New York) in 1928, "admits he gets scared when he has to make a money shot."

Of course, the definition of the phrase—sinking a pressure-packed putt—was much different then, but it remained a regular part of the golfing lexicon up into the 1960s. (It should be noted that it also showed up in a rare basketball, tennis, or even wrestling story.)

Recognizing the meaning today, some of these pre-porn references are worth a chuckle. For instance, in 1969 a *Des Moines Register* columnist named Maury White offered this query about Steve Spray, a consistent-shooting PGA golfer: "Wonder if Old Faithful stroked in the money shot?"

It's quite possible that early X-rated directors appropriated the golfing term, as the timing lines up. Needless to say, while the phrase continued in golf, it lost a lot of its cache after it gained porn prominence. Still, by the 1980s, mainstream Hollywood was comfortable with using the *money shot* to describe any climactic moment. The rest of the world picked it up to reflect a central or key moment by 1990.

> ## "Show me the money!"
> ## —Rod Tidwell (Cuba Gooding Jr.),
> ## *Jerry Maguire* (1996)

Neither *Jerry Maguire*'s writer-director Cameron Crowe nor Cuba Gooding Jr., who uttered the phrase over and over again while playing the flamboyant wide receiver Rod Tidwell, deserve credit for this line. Nope. It was an actual football player named Tim McDonald who coined the phrase.

In doing research for the film, Crowe spent time in 1993 with McDonald, who had just completed a productive six years as a safety with the Arizona Cardinals.

"I said, basically I'm tired of traveling to see all these teams and going through all that talk," McDonald recounted in 1997. "And then I said, given everything I've been through, sooner or later somebody has to show me the money."

As should be expected from a storyteller, the more theatric Crowe, who also penned the film's other culturally resonant lines, "You had me at hello" and "You complete me," remembered the story having a bit more pizzazz.

"He was actually at an owners meeting to be paraded through the lobby to get his price up because he was a free agent," Crowe told a reporter in 1996. "He said, 'I've got a wife and I've got kids and I've been beaten up for five years here in Phoenix and now I'm a free agent. Show me the money.'"

The San Francisco 49ers ultimately did show McDonald the money, giving him a five-year, $12.75 million deal, which was incidentally a bigger deal than Rod Tidwell's fictional four-year, $11.2 million contract in the movie (though not as good of an annual rate).

While the quote quickly became pop-culture fodder with magazines, from *U.S. News & World Report* to *Asiaweek*, using it in cover headlines, one person who grew tired of it was Gooding Jr.

"That line has haunted me ever since," said Gooding, who won an Oscar for the Tidwell role. "I can be at a funeral, in the back you'll hear some (jerk) go, 'Show me the money.'" ★

Munchkin

If you believe MGM lore, you might want to think twice before calling your adorable nephew a *Munchkin*.

That's because the actors who played those cute *Munchkins* in 1939's *The Wizard of Oz* had a dodgy reputation.

"We had a hell of a time with those little guys," the studio's head of production, Mervyn LeRoy, once said. "They got into sex orgies at the hotel. We had to have police on every floor."

But that wasn't all, according to screenwriter Noel Langley. "They raided the [studio] lot," he said. "The showgirls had to be escorted in bunches by armed guards."

Even Dorothy herself, Judy Garland, wasn't kind in her late-life recollections of the *Munchkins*. "They were drunks," she remembered. "They got smashed every night, and the police had to pick them up in butterfly nets."

While that all sounds quite definitive, Aljean Harmetz, who wrote the authoritative book *The Making of The Wizard of Oz*, suggested those assertions might be too harsh. There were 124 *Munchkins* in all, ranging from 2 feet 3 inches to 4 feet 8 inches, and she interviewed a number of them before coming to the conclusion that "the gulf between them and the big people . . . was far less than the big people imagined."

She even went to medical specialists to make the point that while there might have been a few *Munchkins* with big libidos, it's unlikely that they were quite as wild as suggested. Harmetz indicated that those chosen for the film had a hypopituitary disorder, which typically leads to being "not oversexed but undersexed."

Though the truth behind the scenes isn't clear, one thing is certain: The *Munchkins* were loveable on the big screen.

Author L. Frank Baum invented the term (and the fictional people) for his 1900 book on which the movie was based. It caught on early, with the *Oxford English Dictionary* giving an example of a science-fiction writer using Baum's word in 1930, nine years before the movie's release. (*Geek note*: The book had been turned into a silent movie and a play before the Garland-starrer was made.)

But the film's breakaway success deserves credit for the word entering the mainstream as a synonym for a little tyke or someone who is childlike—and eventually, the name for Dunkin' Donuts' addictive doughnut holes. While *Munchkin* is often used as a term of endearment, it can also be pretty derogatory.

For example, Barbara Honegger, who was a political appointee in Ronald Reagan's Justice Department, resigned in 1983 after she said the administration's efforts to combat sex discrimination was a "sham." A Justice Department spokesman responded by calling her a "low-level Munchkin."

Muppet

No matter how cute and loveable Elmo might seem, in many parts of the English-speaking world, being a *muppet* is not a good thing. In the United Kingdom, Ireland, and Australia, the term is slang for a fool or an idiot.

How did these adorable creatures get stamped with such a negative connation?

Before we get there, let's start with the facts behind the invention of the word.

Legendary puppeteer Jim Henson invented the phrase before going on the air with his first show featuring his creatures in 1955. He said it just came to him and claimed he later backfilled with a plausible explanation for its meaning.

"It was really just a term we made up," Henson said. "For a long time I would tell people it was a combination of marionettes and puppets, but basically, it was really just a word that we coined . . . we have done very few things connected with marionettes."

Still, biographer Brian Jay Jones points out that there might have been a subliminal influence in his choice. When Henson lived

Continued on p. 126

> ## "The point is, ladies and gentlemen, that greed, for lack of a better word, is good."
> ### —Gordon Gekko (Michael Douglas), *Wall Street* (1987)

Greed isn't one of the seven deadly sins for nothing. Most hope that when faced with the seduction of such destructive options as sloth, gluttony, wrath . . . or greed, you'd at least take a little pause before diving in.

Hmmmm . . . maybe not so much.

One of those crucible moments came in 1986 when Wall Street executive Ivan Boesky gave the commencement address at the University of California–Berkeley's business school.

"Greed is all right, by the way," he said. "I want you to know that. I think greed is healthy. You can be greedy and still feel good about yourself."

If the comment seems eerily similar to the words of Gordon Gekko, which over the years have been shortened in common conversation to "greed is good," there's a reason. Oliver Stone, who directed and co-wrote the screenplay for *Wall Street*, directly based Gekko's words on Boesky's speech.

Stone said he didn't expect the catchphrase's popularity, and co-writer Stanley Weiser was sure the line would cause disapproving gasps by theater audiences.

"I never could have imagined that this persona and his battle cry would become part of the public consciousness and that the core message of *Wall Street*—remember, he goes to jail in the end—would be so misunderstood by so many," he wrote in the *Los Angeles Times* in 2008.

Weiser certainly had real life to back up this cautionary tale of the downfall of greed. In 1987 Boesky was fined $100 million and sentenced to three years in jail for insider trading. And yet, Weiser might have known better if he'd studied the reaction to Boesky's speech at Berkeley that inspired Stone.

Newsweek explained the crowd's response this way: "The strangest thing, when we come to look back, will be not just that Ivan Boesky could say that at a business-school graduation, but that it was greeted with laughter and applause."

The students failed the deadly sin test, but they did prove (along with so many future scandals on Wall Street) why there's an ongoing fascination with the statement. As Weiser further reflected in 2009: "Greed doesn't come in or out of fashion." ★

in Hyattsville, Maryland, during his teens, there was a children's show that regularly appeared on local TV called *Hoppity, Skippity with Moppet Movies.* A *moppet* has long been a British term for a child and, between the program itself and local advertising, Jones says the term may have been rattling in Henson's brain when he came up with his name.

However it got there, the characters and the word were internationally known in the 1980s when it became derogatory street lingo in the United Kingdom and Ireland.

A simple answer for this transition comes from *The New Partridge Dictionary of Slang and Unconventional English.* Proving everyone's a critic, the book called the Muppets a "gallery of grotesque puppets on which this allusion is founded." In defense of the puppets, the inspiration may have equally been that those being tagged with the *muppet* moniker possessed the same childlike qualities as some of the characters.

Initially, the slang was primarily used as a putdown in jails or as a nickname for police officers. When it came to cops, it doesn't appear that the usage originally had the foolish undertones. But in view of the fact that it was often coming out of the mouths of a criminal element, it's not surprising it quickly became a linguistic slap for mental capacity aimed at people on the force.

While it remains a popular regional phrase, the euphemism got worldwide attention in 2012 when a Goldman Sachs executive wrote a scathing criticism of the investment bank's corporate culture. In a letter that ran in the *New York Times,* he outed five managing directors at the firm for calling their own clients "muppets" on numerous occasions. Following the revelations, the bank went on a "'muppet hunt' to investigate Smith's claims," according to England's *Daily Mail.*

One-night stand
While they had nothing to do with sex, the original *one-night stands* could be cheap and tawdry. The expression started in the music/theater

world to reflect exactly what the phrase suggested: performing for one night at a location and then moving on.

This practice and term existed by the 1870s. Within the next decade there were *one-night stand companies* who played at *one-night stand theaters* all across the United States. The venues could vary greatly, so, like our modern-day *one-night stands*—those casual sexual encounters that come and go—there wasn't a ton of quality control.

The linguistic background to this expression is unmistakably straightforward (a *stand*, as in to take up a position, dates back to the sixteenth century). But how did this phrase become a euphemism for a one-and-done amorous hookup? The first step was a general metaphorical transition for the phrase. In the 1889 classic *A Connecticut Yankee in King Arthur's Court*, Mark Twain used the theatric term to generally mean a quick endeavor. When King Arthur decides he wants to leave the castle in disguise to briefly see how his subjects live, the plan was described as "only a one-night stand."

That might have been enough for the lascivious among us to pick it up for their fleeting dalliances. (The sexual usage was in full swing by the 1930s.) But language expert Martin Harrison believes the connection might be more, ahem, intertwined. He points out in his book *The Language of Theater* that *stand* "has been a colloquial term for the male erection" since at least the sixteenth century. This meaning, he proposes, might have given this phrase a double entendre value that led to its sexual meaning.

Beyond the differing activities each type of *one-night stand* now proposes, you should know that another idiom-inducing expression can be exercised theatrically but lacks the same figurative sex drive. A *one-man show*, which was an early twentieth-century term for a solo variety act and became a general statement for a guy or gal who does it all, still occurs on the stage all the time. As for its bedroom promise, it's fair to say it isn't as great a proposition as the *one-night stand*.

Oscar-worthy

Literally, being *Oscar-worthy* means more than being awarded a thirteen-and-a-half-inch, eight-and-a-half-pound statuette from the Academy of Motion Picture Arts and Sciences. In regular parlance it's applied to just about any act that shows flair or superior performance.

To wit, Hillary Clinton's well-received effort during the first Democratic presidential debates in 2015 was dubbed "Oscar-worthy" by an Examiner.com writer. When the University of Oklahoma Sooners football team unexpectedly stepped up with a strong offensive against Kansas State that year, the local *Norman Transcript* (Oklahoma) dubbed it "an Oscar-worthy acting performance."

Of course, not all references to being Oscar-worthy are sincere. Don't forget, acting does require some artifice.

For example, an exasperated journalist at the *Sun* in Yuma, Arizona, cheekily described the performance of the Siri function on his iPhone in an August 2015 article as "Oscar-worthy" when he asked it to call "Las Palapas Restaurant" and the voice confidently stated it couldn't find a listing for "Last Platypus Restaurant."

For those light on film lore, the reason we all invoke Oscar in these moments likely has to do with a onetime librarian named Margaret Herrick. Officially called the Academy Award of Merit, the statue was originally handed out in 1929. Herrick, who served as the academy's librarian and eventually became the executive director, was said to have casually remarked upon seeing the trophy for the first time in 1931 that it looked like her uncle Oscar. (*Geek note*: The real Uncle Oscar was named Oscar Pierce and was actually Herrick's cousin; he was a well-to-do Texan who made his money growing wheat and fruit.)

The nickname originally hit print in 1934 when Sidney Skolsky made the mention while covering his first Academy Awards for the *New York Daily News*. It's important to note that despite the Herrick story, Skolsky, who would go on to be a prominent syndicated Hollywood gossip columnist, steadfastly claimed paternity for the moniker,

Continued on p. 131

Wasps, Beetles, and Lemurs, Oh My! Animals with Celebrity Names

Asked to give examples of people who leech off stars, we might mention entourages or the paparazzi. But even on the biggest *Family Feud*-style board, we'd never suggest biologists.

Well, survey says, think again.

It's become an increasing habit for scientists who have discovered news species to name them after famous folks—quite often showbiz celebrities. Now, these eminent researchers may actually love the star they've picked as the namesake for an obscure beasty, but it's sometimes about "shameless self-promotion," International Institute for Species Exploration director Quentin Wheeler told *Popular Mechanics* in 2009. Quite frankly, the star appeal can get attention for a discovery that would otherwise be consigned to dry journals. "When you are a taxonomist and are mentioned in *Rolling Stone*, you know you have arrived," Wheeler said.

In actuality, Wheeler probably had his tongue in his cheek (just a bit), as stars often get this honor for work they've done in this space. For instance, John Cleese was the inspiration for a lemur species because of his efforts to protect those animals. Harrison Ford's name was taken for a type of spider as a thank-you for narrating a documentary shot at the London Museum of Natural History (an ant was also reportedly named after Ford for his involvement with Conservation International).

At other times the quest for a celebrity connection can be a bit strained. A 2002 paper about the discovery of twenty-nine new Costa Rican beetle species said one was named after *Titanic* star

Kate Winslet because her "character [in *Titanic*] did not go down with the ship, but we will not be able to say the same for this elegant canopy species if all the rain forest is converted to pastures."

There is an eighteen-chapter International Code of Zoological Nomenclature that sets the rules for this process. But the code gives discoverers enough leeway to provide a lasting shout-out to the person (or thing) of their choosing. Here are some celebrity examples.

- Charlie Chaplin—*Campsicnemus charliechaplini* (fly)
- John Cleese—*Avahi cleesei* (lemur)
- Stephen Colbert—*Aptostichus stephencolberti* (spider) and *Aleiodes colberti* (wasp)
- Ellen DeGeneres—*Aleiodes elleni* (wasp)
- Jimmy Fallon—*Aleiodes falloni* (wasp)
- Harrison Ford—*Calponia harrisonfordi* (spider) and *Pheidole harrisonfordi* (ant)
- Angelina Jolie—*Aptostichus angelinajolieae* (spider)
- Stan Laurel and Oliver Hardy—*Baeturia laureli* and *Baeturia hardyi* (cicadas)
- Jennifer Lopez—*Litarachna lopezae* (aquatic mite)
- Tobey Maguire—*Filistata maguirei* (spider) and *Maguimithrax* (crustacean)
- Arnold Schwarzenegger—*Agra schwarzeneggeri* (beetle) and *Predatoroonops schwarzeneggeri* (spider)
- Liv Tyler—*Agra liv* (beetle)
- Kate Winslet—*Agra katewinsletae* (beetle)

saying he was inspired by an old Vaudeville line, "Will you have a cigar, Oscar?" Whatever the case, the nickname didn't become an official title for the statuette until 1939.

The peanut gallery

Just as sports stadiums have their *cheap seats* or *nosebleed sections*, theaters have historically included the *peanut gallery*. At the highest location of nineteenth-century vaudeville and burlesque venues sat the rowdiest and, generally speaking, the least refined members of the audience. These patrons tended to buy peanuts and did so for two purposes: They were a tasty snack and also could serve as a handy projectile to be aimed at a disappointing act.

The term was regularly used in theater circles by the 1870s. In a story that ran on the front page of an 1874 issue of the *Boston Post*, a theatergoer was rebuffed when looking for a good seat at the New Orleans Varieties Theater before haughtily explaining he was a member of the Mississippi Legislature. This fact snapped the manager to attention: "My dear sir, excuse me! I should as soon think of putting Gen. [Ulysses S.] Grant in the peanut gallery as deny you a front seat in this theater."

There were other terms for folks who took the worst seats at the time. For instance, those in that part of the theater were often called *gallery gods* as they were jokingly closer to the heavens than the stage. But it's *peanut gallery* that has made it all the way into the twenty-first century. One reason for the expression's endurance was its use in the wildly popular TV series *Howdy Doody*, which ran on NBC from 1947 to 1960. An audience of kids was featured prominently and their area was known as the *peanut gallery*. (The big difference: Unlike traditional cheap seats, the kids sat up front.)

The *peanut gallery* idiom for any sort of rowdy or loud group existed by the time *Howdy Doody* took it. In fact, the show's producers probably liked it for that double meaning. Incidentally, *Howdy Doody*'s *peanut gallery* also led to the naming of one of our most beloved comic strips. When cartoonist Charles Schulz was offered a distribution contract from United Feature Syndicate, there was one catch: They required a name change. Schulz called his work *Li'l Folks*, but the syndication company feared it was too similar to the already established *Little Folks* and *Li'l Abner* comics. Inspired by *Howdy Doody*'s *peanut gallery*, they suggested *Peanuts*. Schulz didn't like it but reluctantly agreed.

A few final facts worth noting: The *gallery*, which is synonymous with a theater's upper balconies, developed as a term in the Renaissance era. It also prompted another idiom, *playing to the gallery*, which existed in seventeenth-century England to reflect actors who would *grandstand*—to use a baseball idiom—by overacting in an attempt to appeal to the lesser-paying customers. *Playing to the balcony* is another variation of the expression.

Pratfall

There are all sorts of ways to perform physical comedy. If you want to see a great highlight reel of options, just check out Donald O'Connor's routine to the song "Make 'Em Laugh" in the 1952 film *Singin' in the Rain*. (He gave himself so much to all the bone-bruising gags that it's said he required bed rest after shooting the scene.)

But for all the great moves O'Connor and others have performed, there is clearly one type of fall that rises above the rest in the comic pantheon.

It's landing on your butt.

How do we know this act has a special place in the hearts of audiences? It earned its own special name—the *pratfall*—and then crossed over into the common lexicon.

The key to the term is the word *prat*. While the modern meaning for a *prat* is a fool or an idiot, it was used as far back as the sixteenth century as a word for the derriere. Exactly when it was combined with *fall* to become a slapstick staple is unclear.

The fact that it comes from British slang indicates this talk started in that country, but the book *The Language of Theatre* insists it made its debut in America. References can be found in the 1930s from both British and US sources. In 1932 *Variety* used it as part of a film review for a twenty-one-minute reel called "Who? Me!" That said, the great British actor Noel Coward also mentioned it in 1939.

Either way, two things are clear. The first is that the term quickly broadened in theater and film speak to represent all sorts of falls (not just derriere-centric ones). The second is that it became synonymous with any form of embarrassing mistake or failure by the 1940s. The famed science-fiction writer Ray Bradbury gave the word some additional literary street cred when he wrote in his 1953 classic *Fahrenheit 451*: "Life becomes one big pratfall . . . everything bang, boff, and wow!"

Prima donna

The origin of the title *prima donna* didn't suggest its future meaning for an extravagantly demanding person. The Italian theater applied the term for a principal female singer in an opera from *prima*, meaning first, and *donna*, which literally means woman but surfaced as a seventeenth-century "title of honor or courtesy for an Italian," according to the *Oxford English Dictionary*.

English theater was using it by the end of the 1700s, and it would take on extended meaning in nineteenth-century England to reflect any person of high standing in a community. Charlotte Brontë used the term in that fashion in 1834. But where did the self-important figurative vibe come from? Let's just say when you have a heavenly voice, you can become demanding.

Take Maria Callas, who was one of the great *prima donnas* of the twentieth century. She once told the Vienna State Opera during negotiations: "I'm not interested in money, but it must be more than anyone else." Another time she required the Paris Opera to allow her an unheard-of

Continued on p. 136

"The stuff that dreams are made of."
—Sam Spade (Humphrey Bogart),
The Maltese Falcon (1941)

Like the movie *The Maltese Falcon* itself, the history of this line has the elements of a good film noir: There are unexpected circumstances, mystery, and even some deceit.

The story begins with John Huston looking for his big break. At the time he hadn't directed a movie and thought that Dashiell Hammett's mystery novel *The Maltese Falcon* would be a great source. So he asked his secretary to break down the book scene by scene, using Hammett's dialogue and structure. Huston then planned to ask writer Allen Rivkin to turn it into a screenplay.

But for better or for worse, Warner Bros. studio chief Jack Warner got a hold of the secretary's breakdown and loved it so much, he told Huston he could direct, but rather than an adaptation, he wanted a faithful retelling just as the secretary had laid out. Huston did a bit of trimming and went to work.

The mystery begins here because nowhere in Hammett's book is the line "the stuff that dreams are made of." How it got there has been a trail movie mavens and critics have picked up over the years.

According to film historian William Luhr, the line, which was the final one of the film, was inserted after the original thirty-four days of shooting. Warner wanted a different ending, so Huston reconvened his actors for some additional footage that would give the main character, Sam Spade, more heart than the book provided. This included the final scene and this closing dialogue.

For years, the esteemed director took credit for coming up with the famed line. The motive was clear: The dialogue had become iconic and, while Huston was a much-lauded director by that point, it was a nice garnish on his formidable résumé.

So, case closed, right? Not quite.

Late in life, Huston recanted and gave credit to his leading man Humphrey Bogart, who went from somewhat of a journeyman actor to breakout star with his turn as Spade in this movie.

The line "was Bogie's idea," biographer Lawrence Grobel quoted Huston as saying. "It's been quoted a number of times, but this is the first opportunity I've had to tell where the credit for it lies. Before we shot the scene Bogie said to me, 'John, don't you think it would be a good idea, this line? Be a good ending?' And it certainly was."

Assuming that's true, there is still one more element to tie up. Strong circumstantial evidence points toward William Shakespeare as Bogart's motivation here. In *The Tempest*, the character Prospero talks about how human life is ephemeral: "We are such stuff as dreams are made on, and our little life is rounded with a sleep."

Author Lesley Brill makes the observation that a quote from *A Midsummer Night's Dream* appeared in Hammett's original book but didn't make it into the film. This Shakespearean connection, posits Brill, might have inspired Bogart to paraphrase elsewhere from the great writer's work. ★

twenty or thirty days of rehearsals before performing for them. (Proving *prima donnas* don't always get their way, L'Opera declined.)

In Callas's defense she certainly wasn't the first—or the last—*prima donna* to insist on the fulfillment of lofty desires. The reputation and requirements of opera's lead female singers were well known enough to earn metaphorical status for extreme swagger in Great Britain during the final years of the 1800s.

That usage probably made its way across the Atlantic pretty quickly as the *prima donna* reputation was also notorious in the United States around the same time. A 1916 edition of a publication called *Musical America* asked the following question as part of a humor column: "What made that prima donna demand your discharge?" The punchline: "'I wrote an article,' replied the press agent, 'saying that she sings like an angel. She said she saw no reason for complimentary reference to anybody's singing except her own.'"

As is the case with *drama queens* (p. 59), those bestowing *prima donna* tags don't discriminate based on gender. Among the fellas who have received *prima donna* status from one critic or another in recent years are: Donald Trump (Cher called him that); former *Top Gear* host Jeremy Clarkson (who required, along with many other things, more than twenty bottles of wine, steak knives, and a PlayStation 3 with a copy of *Call of Duty* in his dressing room); and NFL wide receiver Odell Beckham Jr. (by members of an opposing team for not being physical enough).

Now, if you don't like this expression, there's always *diva*, which was in use starting in the late nineteenth century but didn't gain a similar symbolic popularity until well into the second half of the 1900s.

Prop

Sinners attending church services. A descendant of Napoleon Bonaparte. Osama Bin Laden. A fatwa brought on the Pentagon by a Shiite cleric. The vice president in a presidential election campaign. Onetime NBA basketball player Keith Van Horn.

All of these have been described as a *prop* by a journalist at one time or another. The media, often cynically, loves twisting this theater term to represent just about any person, place, or thing that's either being used to illustrate a point or is taking the role of useless window dressing.

Actual *props* date back to at least the ancient Greeks. The original prop masters were people known as *skeuopoios*, who made masks and other objects that were taken onstage. In English the term *prop* is shorthand for *stage property*, which by the 1420s became the name for an item used in a performance. At the time of Elizabeth I's reign during the following century, the wide variety of available *props* were already impressive. They could include musical instruments, weapons and armor, feathers, skins of beasts, coffins, chariots, and boars' heads.

Over time *prop* language grew more specific. There are *personal props* that are specific to one character and *hand props* that are carried. The *prop table* sits in the theater wings with pieces that will be brought on and off the stage. (If you're wondering, *props*, as in giving respect, didn't start in the theater; it's a slang shortening for the word *proper*.)

When it comes to the person who must corral all these items, the pressure—whether it be in a theater or film production—can be heavy. For example, one late morning during the shooting of the 1936 film *The Trail of the Lonesome Pine*, director Henry Hathaway asked his prop master Oscar Lau to get a bouquet of flowers for a scene after lunch. The problem was the movie was being shot in the middle of the California desert. Undeterred, Lau jumped in a car and sped to the closest outpost of humanity, Mojave, which was quite a distance away.

Fresh flowers would be nearly impossible to find in the small town, but he knew a train passed through to pick up water around midday. He got there just in time to slip $10 to a steward, who allowed him to take flowers from the dining room. Much to the surprise of everyone on the production, he returned in time with the necessary *prop*.

While Lau's flowers are long gone, many other *props* have earned artifact status and are highly sought after by collectors. For example, Luke Skywalker's lightsaber from the original *Star Wars* was once sold for $240,000, while a proton pack from *Ghostbusters 2* brought in $130,000.

Putting on an act

Putting on an act was the first step toward a cottage industry of *act*-based idioms. Clearly, the word *act*, which dates back to the 1500s as a way to describe performing, is essential to showbiz. We all know that it's pretty hard to have a play, film, or TV show without *act*ors or *act*resses.

But *putting on an act* is a much more recent development. It came from vaudeville, where an *act* was a late nineteenth-century term of art for an individual or a team of performers that took part in the variety productions. Some experts suggest that an *act* in this sense was taken from the already-established use of the word to represent a section of a play (similar to legit theater's intermissions, there was typically a brief break between each troupe's arrival on stage; see *second act*, p. 144). But this might be overthinking it, as the term could have simply been a shortening of the word *acting*, which is, of course, what these performers were doing.

From there, *putting on an act* emerged in the opening decade of the 1900s as industry-speak for mounting a theater routine. (Example: "The jugglers are putting on an act at the Palladium.") This being vaudeville, many of these acts could be excessive and, in some cases, hard to believe. Hence, we were teed up for its metaphorical use to reflect acting in an insincere manner.

Still, the expression didn't appear to go idiomatic until the 1920s. It showed up as part of a book serialization by Eleanor Early called *The Shining Talent* that ran in newspapers across the United States in 1929.

(It would be repackaged as a book called *Love's Denial* in 1932.) At one point in the story, the main character, Molly, tries to convince a couple that she comes from modest means. When they don't believe her, Molly replies, "I'm not putting on an act! . . . I'm telling you the truth."

Once that expression entered the firmament, the *act* imagery became a springboard for other figures of speech. Next up was *a hard act to follow*, which can be found by the late 1930s to mean a person or thing that is difficult to match or surpass. *Getting in on the act* emerged as a synonym for getting involved in the 1940s and 1950s, and *cleaning up one's act* got traction in the 1960s (there was surely enough questionable behavior in that decade to warrant the phrase).

The most recent addition is *getting one's act together*, which was established in the 1970s. The timing here also makes sense as the people who were *cleaning up their act* just years before now needed a way to tell loved ones they were taking care of their problems.

Quickie

The first *quickie* took place in Hollywood, and for you naughty-minded folks, no, it didn't happen on a casting couch. The word first emerged no later than 1926 to describe movies that were done in about fifteen days, on the cheap, and often with big-name actors.

"Hollywood is in the throes of the 'quickies,'" wrote one of the film industry's best-known gossip columnists, Louella Parsons, in 1927. "This illegitimate offspring of the more dignified feature production manages to get some of our best players."

Parsons reported that these movies were so popular among filmmakers of all stripes because they were financial gold mines. The key was getting top-shelf actors, who would take the jobs for a nice paycheck. This could be done because the filmmakers would skimp on other elements and simply sell the movie on the names of their big stars.

These pictures could cost as little $40,000 (or around $545,000 in modern terms) and would provide returns no less than $200,000 ($2.7

Continued on p. 142

> ## "There's no place like home."
> ## —Dorothy (Judy Garland),
> ## *The Wizard of Oz* (1939)

This quote is pretty unique among the great lines in film history because it's so closely tied to the film and, yet, it's completely derivative of another unconnected work. (Though see "The stuff that dreams are made of," on p. 134, for another potential example.) The phrase "be it ever so humble, there's no place like home" was the closing line of the 1823 song "Home, Sweet Home" by lyricist John Howard Payne and composer Sir Henry Bishop.

Originally written for a British melodrama called *Clari, or the Maid of Milan,* "Home, Sweet Home" was such a big hit that it was widely beloved in the United States by the time the Civil War commenced. Case in point: In 1862, on the eve of a battle near Murfreesboro, Tennessee, the Union and Confederate forces, separated by just seven hundred yards, each began singing the song. Abraham Lincoln was such a fan that he asked Italian opera star Adelina Patti to perform it at the White House.

L. Frank Baum, who wrote the 1900 novel *The Wonderful Wizard of Oz,* was almost certainly aware of the tune and made what appeared to be a passing nod to it in his book. At one point early in their travels, the Scarecrow asks Dorothy about her home and why she wants to return.

Dorothy replies: "No matter how dreary and gray our homes are, we people of flesh and blood would rather live there than in any other country, be it ever so beautiful. There is no place like home."

Though the line wasn't central in the book, the film elevated its status. Screenwriters Florence Ryerson and Edgar Allan Woolf deserve credit for actually putting the "'there's no place like home' motif" into the shooting script, according to *Wizard of Oz* expert Aljean Harmetz.

But behind the scenes, it was likely MGM executive Arthur Freed who pushed for the emphasis on the expression. During the development of the script, he wrote a memo to Ryerson and Woolf emphasizing the importance of the actual words. (Spoiler alert: Dorothy ultimately needed to click her ruby slippers three times and say the magic phrase to herself to return to Kansas in the film.)

As for the film's multitude of other great lines—"Toto, I've got a feeling we're not in Kansas anymore"; "I'll get you my pretty, and your little dog too"; "Lions and tigers and bears, oh my"; "I'm melting! Melting! Oh, what a world! What a world!"; and "Pay no attention to the man behind the curtain"—none of them appear in Baum's book.

However, assessing credit for their big-screen creation isn't easy. A total of *ten* screenwriters helped develop the film's script. That said, Noel Langley probably played the most essential role in forming the dialogue. He received first billing among the three credited writers, with Ryerson and Woolf being the other two. ★

million today), according to Parsons. Not surprisingly, big players of the time dabbled in these projects. For example, both Charlie Chaplin and Harold Lloyd were invested to varying degrees in the *quickie* business.

Nobody in Hollywood has been credited with popularizing the name (maybe that's because nobody wanted to be too closely associated with a quickie—at least not in a film sense. Of course, it's possible somebody from an earlier time created the term. The word *quick* to mean moving with speed is ancient, with references dating back to at least the fourteenth century. This means the innovation of adding an "ie" seems like it could have been done a time long before the movie business did it.

Still, what does appear clear is that the Hollywood meaning predated using the word as a euphemism for a speedy intimate dalliance or even a one-and-out nightcap at your local bar.

As to whether Hollywood influenced those other meanings, you should never underestimate the power of Parsons's pen. In 1927 her column was syndicated nationally and papers in towns from Abilene, Texas, to Charleston, West Virginia, picked up this story. This means it's quite possible that the movie *quickie* was a well-known entity to whoever started using the word for other purposes.

Ride off into the sunset

From a practical and unromantic standpoint, having the hero *ride off into the sunset* is an odd plan. Wouldn't you want to leave at dawn to get the most amount of time on the road before setting up camp? Of course, movies and TV are all about suspending disbelief, so rather than harp on the practical, that timely ride served as a metaphor: Just as the sun was departing, the movie (or TV/radio show) was ending.

This concept was such an integral part of cowboy films that in the late 1930s it was already as worn out as an old saddle. "Western addicts, more resentful of change than any of the other [movie] customers, still demand that Tex or Buck or Larry ride off into the sunset astride his faithful mount," sniffed *New York Times* journalist Douglas W. Churchill in 1938. The following year Churchill continued to complain about the formula, pointing out in a mocking tone that the hero "must ride into the sunset with only a light promise, carelessly given, of returning some day when he wants to settle down and be a foreman of the ranch."

No matter, Hollywood moguls kept embracing the cliché. Still, from a linguistic perspective, they cannot take credit for creating the phrase. An 1898 issue of a British magazine called *The Co-operative News* used it when providing a description of the tiny pixie Ariel from William Shakespeare's *The Tempest*. "This spirit was very clever, and told all the other spirits what to do," the magazine said, "though he was so small that he could sleep in a cowslip bell, and ride into the sunset on the bat's back."

Even if *The Co-operative News* (and likely others) got there first, Westerns spurred this defining idiom for a happy ending. Though nowadays, it's sometimes used to merely reflect the end of the road. When longtime New York Giants football coach Tom Coughlin opted to resign in 2016 after three straight losing seasons, a Fox Sports analyst said Coughlin would "ride off in the sunset." He did lead his club to two previous Super Bowl championships, but it had been a while since he'd played an NFL hero.

Riding off into the sunset remains a popular expression, but it's not the only contribution these *horse operas*, as they've often been called, have given to the English language. Along with *Get out of Dodge* (see p. 75), others include: *cut them* (or *head 'em*) *off at the pass* as a way to say you're aiming to beat someone or something to a vital point; *black hats* and *white hats* to represent bad and good guys, respectively; *circling the wagons* for taking a defensive posture; and *meanwhile, back at the ranch*, which was once a popular way to suggest a segue in a conversation, were all phrases popularized by Western films and TV and radio shows.

Rolling in the aisles

If language is our guide, the aisles are where any comedic theatrical troupe wants its audience to end up. You are looking to either have them *rolling in the aisles* or be able to *knock them* and/or *lay them in the aisles* if you're doing it correctly.

Surprisingly, the metaphor's inspiration may have come from the literal practice of aisle-rolling at another type of performance: the church. In 1915 a Trenton, New Jersey, paper reported that a preacher "grew indignant when he saw a youngster disturbing attention in the rear of the citadel by rolling in one of the aisles." Two years later the *Atlanta Constitution* offered a more positive spin on the activity, saying a service was "so marvelous [with] the power of God that gray-haired old blasphemers fell on their knees, others rolled in the aisles, and they cried out, 'Oh, spare us!'"

Maybe that image inspired the entertainment industry. Either way, in the 1920s show business embraced the importance of aisles—whether it be rolling, knocking, or laying 'em in them. It was new enough in 1923 that the *Illustrated Daily News* in Los Angeles relied on a clarifying modifier when using the idiom in a positive review of a revue. "These lads had us metaphorically rolling in the aisle long before the proper time for that impropriety," the critic said.

Within the next two decades, all types of speakers were figuratively aiming to crowd the aisles with their oratory. The author P. G. Wodehouse wrote in his 1940 book *Quick Service*: "I made the speech of a lifetime. I had them tearing up the seats and rolling in the aisles." It would ultimately branch out even further to reflect pleasure with all sorts of activities. An example: In 1959 the *New York Times* said that the young gazelles at the Bronx Zoo were so cute they had "men rolling in the aisles."

Second act
Take note that from a classical perspective, getting to a *second act* still means you have a long way to go. When it came to tragedies, the Romans did things in *five* acts. (Apparently, Aristotle misstated how

the Greeks traditionally handled the structure of the genre, hence the five Roman acts.)

Over time, that lengthy commitment was pared down with many seventeenth- and eighteenth-century writers opting for three acts (though four-act plays gained some popularity in the 1800s). In the twentieth century, the rise of a single intermission—aka two-act plays—paved the way for this metaphor.

In particular, F. Scott Fitzgerald is remembered for his connection to the *second act* as a synonym for a comeback. It's famously included in his book *The Last Tycoon*, which was published posthumously in 1941. The line goes, "there are no second acts in American lives."

Now, if you ponder the scores of politicians (Bill Clinton), athletes (George Foreman), and captains of industry (Steve Jobs) who have enjoyed metaphorical *second acts*, Fitzgerald's observation deserves some criticism.

But supporters of the beloved author are quick to point out that Fitzgerald had previously applied the phrase in a different light for an essay called *My Lost City* about the resilience of New York City. His full statement in that work, which was written around 1932, was: "I once thought that there were no second acts in American lives, but there was certainly to be a second act to New York's boom days." As a result, maybe Fitzgerald, who was always looking for his own *second act* after penning the great American novel *The Great Gatsby*, got it.

While Fitzgerald's use solidified the second-chance meaning for this expression, a *second act* was already percolating figuratively in the lexicon. The *New York Times*, for instance, used it in a 1924 story on foreign relations. The August 6 edition that year said, "Thanks to the moderation and cordiality of the German Chancellor the second act of the London conference opened auspiciously."

Another similar expression, the *final act*, as in the last period of your life, is a bit more muddled in its lineage. Denizens of the stage

Continued on p. 148

> ## "What we've got here is failure to communicate."
> —Captain (Strother Martin),
> *Cool Hand Luke* (1967)

Donn Pearce penned the book on which *Cool Hand Luke* was based and took a first crack at the screenplay. When the producers didn't appreciate Pearce's cinematic efforts, they hired Frank Pierson to revamp it. Pierson included this line—often misstated as "What we have here is a failure to communicate"—but worried it wasn't quite right.

"I thought it sounded like something a highly educated person would say and that everybody involved with the movie would ask how this Southern redneck could say something that has a certain smell of academia," Pierson said about the line that was uttered to the rebellious convict Luke, played by Paul Newman. "But nobody ever questioned [it]. Strother Martin got it right away and said it perfectly."

Pierson, who was nominated alongside Pearce for a best adapted screenplay Oscar, once said that he didn't have any specific inspiration for the quote, but more than forty years after he came up with the famous words, he could remember exactly where and how it happened.

"I was typing on my old Underwood in my house overlooking the sea in Malibu," he told the *Los Angeles Times* in 2010. "In the scene, Luke has been recaptured and the warden wants to teach him a lesson. This whole thing has to do with getting Luke's mind right. And suddenly it materialized on the page in front of me."

L.A. Times journalist Donald Liebenson suggested the quote resonated immediately because "it came to crystallize 1960s discontent and the generation gap."

It certainly has proved enduring over the years as versions of the statement have showed up in an amazingly diverse number of TV shows, films, and songs. Those include: the animated series *Rugrats*, movies as different as the Kevin Costner action drama *Waterworld* and the broad Jim Varney comedy *Ernest Saves Christmas*, and the Guns N' Roses song "Civil War."

Despite that universal appreciation, there was one person who disliked both the movie and this famed phrase: the original author Pearce, whose own life included a stint on a chain gang just like the one dramatized in the movie.

"I seem to be the only guy in the United States who doesn't like the movie," Pearce said in 1989. "Everyone had a whack at it. They screwed it up ninety-nine different ways."

In 2007 his salty attitude hadn't diminished—especially when talking about Pierson's signature line.

"I hated it," he told the *Palm Beach Post* (Florida). "I don't believe in tag lines. I think artistically they're extremely poor. I don't give a damn if it's 'Pucker up and whistle' or 'Round up the usual suspects' or 'Play it again, Sam.' At best it just drips with sentimentality and in this instance, it was snide and untrue and unrealistic."

For what it's worth, Pearce got a bit of redemption in 2015 when the Godlight Theater Company in New York City did a production of *Cool Hand Luke* that was faithful to the original book. Noticeably missing in the script: "What we've got here is failure to communicate." ★

may have devised it, but it should be said that an *act* has been a legal term to describe a document or decree since at least the 1300s, and calling a formal summary of a conference a *final act* has its own history from there. In addition, a *final act*, as in a last action, could also have inspired this idiom.

Set the stage

In the early days of theater, literally *setting the stage* (or performing its linguistic cousin, *setting the scene*) wasn't such a big deal.

The writer Marcus Vitruvius Pollio explained the straightforward details of erecting a stage during the Roman era in his book series *De Architectura*, which was written between 16 and 13 BCE.

"There are three kinds of scenes," he wrote. "One called the tragic, second, the comic, third the satyric."

The basic troika was erected on a triangular piece of machinery that could be rotated depending on the genre of the production. In case you want to know how the stage should be set for the varying events in your life, the decorations for each panel were simple and thematic. Tragedies had "columns, pediments, statues and other objects suited to kings." Comedies featured "private dwellings, with balconies and views representing rows of windows, after the manner of ordinary dwellings." When it was time for satire, Pollio said you should go with "trees, caverns, mountains, and other rustic objects delineated in landscape style."

Needless to say, we've upped production values over the years.

In medieval Europe, for example, a 1493 Florentine production of a religious play called *sacra rappresentazione*, featured a massive contraption to set the stage. The apparatus, created by architect Filippo Brunelleschi, was dazzling, with scores of lights and harnesses so that twelve children dressed as little cherubs could dangle in the background.

It was common practice for British theaters to put up just one painted scene as an all-purpose background in productions during most of the eighteenth century (this was known as *stock scenery*). The exception was London theater manager John Rich, who innovated the practice of switching out backgrounds regularly by the 1720s.

During the late nineteenth century, actor and theater manager Sir Herbert Beerbohm Tree took it to the next level in his London West End productions of Shakespeare. His version of *Twelfth Night* had carpets of real grass. *The Winter's Tale* featured an actual running stream and waterfall, and rabbits could be seen bounding about onstage amidst *A Midsummer Night's Dream*.

Still, as anybody who's ever had to begrudgingly listen to a friend who overdid it while *setting the scene* for a story, sometimes less can be more.

In 1949 the Broadway production of *Death of a Salesman* went with a design that never required switching out scenery, despite the fact that the play took place in multiple locations. Instead, there was very little put on the stage, and actors brought props on and off as the play progressed. The spartan approach was lauded, and set designer Jo Mielziner won a Tony Award for his work in creating that stage.

As far as using the expressions *set the scene* or *set the stage* as idiomatic preparation for a future event or anecdote, those were in use by the late nineteenth century.

Showboat
If you were transported back to the 1830s and saw the first-ever *showboat*, you'd be astonished that it paved the way for a term used to describe a show-off.

William Chapman Sr. was a British actor who came to the United States to ply his trade. He started in New York and Philadelphia before heading out west to Pittsburgh. The Steel City proved to be an uninviting theatrical town, so Chapman came up with another plan: Create a stage on a boat and head downriver to New Orleans, stopping along the way to put on performances.

His initial ship, named *The Floating Theatre*, was anything but ostentatious. It was a flat boat said to be a slender-but-long fourteen by one hundred feet. It had no engine, featured a small stage and rudimentary wooden benches for patrons, and was designed in a way that once it reached its final destination, it could be broken down and sold for kindling wood.

When he started these voyages in 1831, Chapman had a lot going for him. Communities downriver were thirsting for entertainment, and the Mississippi had just added a number of channels, making the trip safer and faster. Nevertheless, it was hard work, as Chapman and his family—the company included nine family members and two others—would get up at three a.m. every day to move from one location to the next and set up the evening's production on the ship. Round-trip, each journey (in which the family would return to Pittsburgh via stage coach or steamer after arriving in New Orleans) took a year.

Still, it was a very successful venture, and after five times down the river and back, the Chapmans had enough money to purchase a proper steamer, which they named *The Floating Palace*, complete with backdrops and legit seating. William Chapman died around 1841, and the family would ultimately leave the business. But by then there were scores of *showboats* traveling the Mississippi and Ohio Rivers.

The Civil War diminished the popularity of this form of entertainment. But after the hostilities ended, more elaborate ships became popular. Initially, folks like the Chapmans did serious theater (for instance, Shakespeare), but the entertainment on the fancy postwar boats hammed it up with over-the-top melodramas and vaudeville acts.

That later extravagant excitement was captured in Edna Ferber's 1926 novel *Show Boat*. Ferber's book was a hit, but the subsequent musical by Jerome Kern and Oscar Hammerstein likely cemented the figurative usage.

In 1951, when a very successful version of the musical was released on the big screen, the *showboat* as genre of theater had basically been

Continued on p. 152

A Jumbo Entertainer: P. T. Barnum

A good showman knows how to talk. Since P. T. Barnum declared himself the "Greatest Showman on Earth"—and many agreed—it's not surprising that he was an expert at finding just the right words.

Indeed, Barnum, a talented circus impresario who also did so many other things—including running a museum of curiosities and promoting the great Swedish opera singer Jenny Lind—is the first-known person to use the terms *bandwagon* and *sideshow* in print. Both showed up in his 1855 autobiography and were applied metaphorically by the end of the century (*bandwagon* for suddenly showing support for a succeeding enterprise, and *sideshow* for any sort of minor issue, matter, or event).

In addition, Barnum popularized the expressions *jumbo* and *Siamese twins*. In 1882 Jumbo was the largest elephant in captivity at the time. The animal was the property of the London Zoological Garden, but Barnum purchased him for a reported $10,000. He made Jumbo, whose name became synonymous with *superlarge* (as any self-respecting McDonald's patron would know), such a great attraction that after the pachyderm died in 1885, Barnum stuffed the animal and preserved his bones so the showman could continue to reap profits.

Siamese twins developed into the common term for conjoined siblings because of Eng and Chang Bunker. The brothers were born in what is modern-day Thailand (hence, the Siamese reference) and rose to fame as part of Barnum's circus. They eventually toured on their own, making enough money to buy land in North Carolina.

For all he gave, Barnum isn't the only one from the circus world who has bestowed useful expressions upon us. For instance, the dead for at least a decade. Nevertheless, around then the expression had gained steam, so to speak, assuring that the legacy of the Chapmans' work would remain vibrant—in the English language, at least.

Sixty-four thousand dollar ($64,000) question

The world changed monumentally between 1940 and 1955. We fought a world war, came home, and, for the most part, entered into those comfortable post-WW II years. But amongst the biggest shifts in that period was the value of the largest colloquial question you could ask.

At the start of the 1940s, if you posed a *$64 question*, you were asking something tough. By the mid-1950s it was going to take a *$64,000 question* to really stump somebody.

The source of both of these queries can be found in the CBS radio quiz show *Take It or Leave It*, which premiered on April 21, 1940. The way it worked was a contestant would get a $1 question. If the person got it right, he or she could continue, answering up to six more increasingly difficult offerings. While the player could stop at any time, with each correct answer, he or she would double their winnings. (That's how we got to the seemingly arbitrary $64 sum.)

Simple in concept, the program was a big hit, and people from all walks of life began employing the catchphrase from the show: *That's the $64 question*. Outside of the program, the $64 tag wasn't always applied to the toughest of questions. For example, an April 1942 report from Anderson, Indiana, in *The Typographical Journal*, which was the official paper of the International Typographical Union, asked, "The $64 question" about who attended a dinner in Chicago.

While $64 was an okay haul in 1940 (as a point of comparison, the average rent for a New York City apartment in that decade was $50 a month), it wasn't enough for the first golden age of television. *Take It or Leave It* left the radio waves in 1948, but seven years later CBS rebooted it for television with much bigger bucks at stake. *The $64,000 Question* was considered the first "big money" game show. It was America's most popular program in the 1955–56 TV season, even outrating *I Love Lucy*, and ran until 1958.

The increased price of a thorny question—$64,000 back then had the value of more than $500,000 today—was enough to give the phrase some long-term currency. Everyone from US Sen. Charles Schumer to TV news personality Greta Van Susteren has used it in recent years.

For those of you who feel shortchanged, the concept of a *million-dollar question* is a relatively venerable alternative. That usage can be found since at least the early 1920s. In fact, Hollywood was an early adopter of that option. In a 1922 advertisement in the *Taylor Daily Press* (Texas) for director Lois Weber's movie *What Do Men Want?*, the ad describes the film's title as "The Million Dollar Question."

Smoke and mirrors

Magic has long had its own language. While the phrase *sleight of hand* was in the English lexicon by the 1400s to generally describe manual dexterity, it wasn't until the 1600s that it took on the meaning of trickery. During the seventeenth century two other magic-related phrases still used today to varying degrees—*abracadabra* and *hocus pocus*—also existed.

But the big illusion, like those that inspired *smoke and mirrors* as an idiom for all sorts of misleading acts, didn't really exist before the 1800s when scientific progress ushered in the era of modern magic. In the 1840s a Paris clockmaker named Jean Eugène Robert-Houdin opened

Continued on p. 156

> ## "Why don't you come up sometime and see me?"
> ## —Lady Lou (Mae West),
> ## *She Done Him Wrong* (1933)

Mae West knew her brand. She was a bawdy, curvaceous, smart, and strong lady. It was a persona she controlled every step of the way. For example, when she had her first big hit on Broadway, *Diamond Lil*, which was about a dance hall hostess-singer in New York's hardscrabble Bowery in the 1890s, she fought throughout to maintain creative authority.

When Hollywood came calling to do a big-screen adaptation, West was equally commanding. For the film, which was called *She Done Him Wrong*, she fired the original screenwriter, John Bright, and replaced him with Harvey Thew. She also battled with director Lowell Sherman and personally picked then-up-and-comer Cary Grant as the leading man. The effort was worth the results. The movie, released February 9, 1933, was a success, earning a best picture Oscar nomination and providing this breakout piece of dialogue.

Well, sort of.

In actuality, the line that people have mimicked for decades is "Why don't you come up and see me sometime?" And while many point out it's a misquote of her words from *She Done Him Wrong*, West still deserves credit for perfecting—and emphasizing her connection—to what would become her catchphrase.

You see, West wrote her next film, *I'm No Angel*, which was released just eight months later, in October, and being attuned to the buzz from *She Done Him Wrong*, she delivered "come up and see me sometime" in that film's dialogue. (Geek note: It's unlikely that modifying the verbiage bothered West a bit; she had already used variations on this line even before *Diamond Lil* and *She Done Him Wrong*.)

West's efforts with these words gave her the intended result. A movie called *Take a Chance* bowed in November 1933 and featured actress Lillian Roth singing a racy song called "Come Up and See Me Sometime," which was likely inspired by the already popular West quote and was eventually recorded by West herself.

"Every dinner party has a Mae West imitator," wrote O. O. McIntyre in a December 1933 edition of his nationally syndicated column about life in New York City. "All it requires is a hand on the hip and a whiney: 'Why don't you come up to see me sometime?'" ★

a magic theater and is widely credited with the shift to jaw-dropping tricks and effects on the stage. (*Geek note*: The great magician Harry Houdini took his stage name from Robert-Houdin.)

Well versed in emerging scientific wonders that most patrons weren't savvy about, Robert-Houdin astounded audiences. For instance, he utilized magnets in a trick involving a trunk. He'd get a burly audience member to come up and easily lift an empty box. The magician would then stealthily flip a switch engaging some magnets to make it impossible for the same man to get the trunk to budge from the floor.

Other big, well-planned deceptions would use *smoke and mirrors* to bend perception and wow onlookers. These were commonplace well into the twentieth century. However, it took quite a while for a high-profile writer to take what had become a piece of stock-and-trade magic as a metaphor.

That person was the Pulitzer Prize–winning journalist Jimmy Breslin. In his 1975 book *How the Good Guys Finally Won: Notes from Impeachment Summer*, Breslin relied on the concept more than once. Most notably, he wrote: "The ability to create the illusion of power, to use mirrors and blue smoke, is one found in unusual people."

Although he didn't exactly coin the phrase, a book reviewer turned it around and, possibly, started it down the road to its modern construction. Amusingly, the critic Martin F. Nolan, who was a longtime *Boston Globe* reporter, made the reference while criticizing Breslin's prowess at weaving analogies.

"Breslin's skill is with people. It is not with extended metaphors," Nolan wrote in his 1975 *New York Times* review. "Throughout the book several metaphors lumber into view. Blue smoke and mirrors are used. . . ." The general public has unmistakably disagreed with Nolan's perspective, as *smoke and mirrors* became a popular idiom by the early 1980s.

One final metaphor to note from this art: *pulling a rabbit out of a hat*. Like *smoke and mirrors*, the phrase was slow to develop a figurative meaning. It was a trick by the early decades of the 1800s, but it wasn't used to describe achieving surprising success until the twentieth century.

Sneak preview

There was a time when getting a seat at a *sneak preview* gave you a lot of power. Today, we think of *sneak previews* as an early opportunity to see a finished product or, sometimes, an early teaser of an upcoming picture. The film industry uses the expression in that way, as do people in other walks of life, from Defense Department briefings to high-fashion presentations.

But when the phrase emerged in the 1930s, a cinematic *sneak preview* was what we now call a *test screening* (a term that didn't come about, at least publicly, until the 1940s). As syndicated columnist and sometime Hollywood producer Mark Hellinger (*The Naked City*) described these viewings in a 1939 article: "A sneak preview is a most mysterious event, staged by the producers of a picture before the film is ready for the public. In other words, it's a sort of test performance to which nobody is invited—and everybody shows up."

The creator of the phrase and the activity is a matter for debate. A 1935 *New York Times* article credited legendary director Cecil B. DeMille with its "invention." But the same paper gave another prominent producer of that age, Irving Thalberg, the recognition in 1982. In 2005 the *Village Voice* noted that successful comedy actor–filmmaker Harold Lloyd was a "pioneer" of this practice by 1928.

Whoever deserves the praise, *sneak previews* were known nation-wide by 1932. That year newspapers from spots as varied as Tyrone, Pennsylvania, and San Antonio, Texas, were running articles about the phenomenon. (If you're wondering, *sneak peek* can be found in print by the 1940s, but it isn't clear if the movie industry spurred the phrase, which wasn't initially used in cinema-related instances.)

For directors—and movie lovers—these proceedings have long been considered a mixed bag.

"If the screenings are used by filmmakers themselves to get feedback on a rough cut, that's valid," the esteemed film critic Roger Ebert wrote in 2004. "Too often, however, studio executives use preview screenings as a weapon to enforce their views on directors. . . ."

Ebert pointed to how director Billy Wilder decided to recut the first reel of the classic film *Sunset Boulevard* after a test screening as an example of a *sneak preview*'s upside. On the other hand, there are numerous instances when the test audience gave off a decidedly incorrect vibe about a film. Most notably, the producers of *The Wizard of Oz* nearly cut the film's signature song "Over the Rainbow" after a disagreeable *sneak preview*.

Soap opera

In 1947 the *New York Times* quoted a New Jersey official who made the amazing claim that *soap operas* helped save lives.

"Fatigue is an important factor in home accidents," said Grace Hornaday, who was secretary of the Women's Division of the Newark (New Jersey) Safety Council. "In fact, a tired housewife is an accident waiting to happen. I believe in the necessity for occasional relaxation so strongly that I think even soap operas serve a useful purpose if they bring a pause in the day's occupation for the overtired housewife."

Okay, that's the type of overcooked declaration that you'd hear *on* a *soap opera* rather than *about* a *soap opera*, but the statement did speak to how the genre of radio shows—it wouldn't hit TV until the 1950s—had become part of the cultural bedrock in less than twenty years.

The *soap opera* format emerged at the beginning of the 1930s as a daytime staple on local and national radio. The target audience was women at home during the day, and soap companies lined up to sponsor this popular programming in the hopes of luring them to their products.

In the early days these radio dramas were generally called "strip shows" or simply "serials." Referring to them as *soap operas* (in reference to the ubiquitous sponsors) emerged at the end of the 1930s. *Newsweek* used the nickname in November of 1939, and a month later the *Washington Post* ran an article referring to actors on the shows as "soap opera hams."

The name was probably inspired by the movies. The idea of cheekily combining opera with another word to describe a plot style existed with Western films, which were commonly called *horse operas* by the 1920s. (Today we also have *space opera* to describe sci-fi epics like the *Star Wars* franchise.)

Ruminating on the *soap opera*'s success, one journalist said the key from the very beginning was to make sure that the listener was always compelled to return.

"The underlying idea is not to present and develop a situation, provide it with a climax and bring it to a fitting conclusion, as in a play or novel," wrote a critic in a 1940 edition of the *Washington Post*. "Plays and novels end, but the soap operas go on forever, or until they are junked by the sponsor."

Even if you weren't a fan, you couldn't help but recognize that *soap operas* had become synonymous with often-absurd drama—a fact that allowed for the phrase's easy transition into everyday discussions about life before the end of the 1940s.

In 1944 the crime writer Raymond Chandler used it in this fashion in his book *The Lady in the Lake*. A character in the mystery lamented about an ex-lover who left him, then thanked the main character, the renowned detective Philip Marlowe, "for listening to the soap opera."

Song and dance

Like cookies and cream or bacon and eggs, *song and dance* just go together. While the *Oxford English Dictionary*'s earliest reference to the combo dates to 1628, it's easy to assume that using the two words in tandem (along with the entertaining activity) span much further back in time.

Continued on p. 161

A Rose by Any Other Name: Arranging Showbiz Flora

When Barbra Streisand had a rose named after her in 2001, she insisted it be fragrant. TV chef extraordinaire Julia Child had a say in choosing the butter-yellow hue and licorice candy smell for her namesake rose.

Cultivators introduce new roses every year, and whether it's through direct involvement (Oprah Winfrey played a part in the design of one) or just inspiration, the entertainment business has long been a horticulture magnet.

Literally speaking, the greatest Hollywood rose is probably the Ingrid Bergman (some may make the figurative argument as well). Unveiled in 1984, the red hybrid tea rose has won numerous prizes, including the Award of Garden Merit from England's Royal Horticultural Society; it was also inducted into the Rose Hall of Fame by the World Federation of Rose Societies. The list of stars who have lent their names to roses is broad, from George Burns and Henry Fonda to Dolly Parton and Betty White.

Still, some are better than others, as is always the case in *showbiz* (a phrase that incidentally spawned its own flower; see below). The following is a list of entertainment industry–inspired roses, along with their types and colors, that have been named All-American Rose Selections (AARS), which is a bit like winning a gardening Oscar.

- Jiminy Cricket, 1955 (floribunda, coral orange)
- Roman Holiday, 1967 (floribunda, orange/red)
- Bing Crosby, 1981 (hybrid tea, orange)
- Showbiz, 1985 (floribunda, scarlet)

- Broadway, 1986 (hybrid tea, reddish pink)
- All That Jazz, 1992 (shrub, orange/yellow)
- Brigadoon, 1992 (hybrid tea, yellow)
- Singin' in the Rain, 1995 (floribunda, coppery orange)
- Betty Boop, 1999 (floribunda, yellow/red)
- Julia Child, 2006 (floribunda, golden yellow)
- Dick Clark, 2011 (grandiflora, creamy white/burgundy)

But around the 1860s, the phrase really developed into a term of art for a specific form of entertainment in the United States. A *song-and-dance man* or *song-and-dance performer* would sing some songs, tell some jokes, and do a tap or soft-shoe dance routine. The finale would typically include some breathtaking dance tricks. (A 1911 history of some of these acts would make note when a performer was "acrobatic.") Speaking to the times, this was all often done in blackface.

They were well-received acts, and when vaudeville troupes and traveling minstrel shows came to town, they'd promote this style of performance. For example, in 1867, the *Piqua Democrat* (Ohio) referred to one performer in Newcomb's Minstrels as "the greatest song and dance man in the work."

The elaborate nature—and nationwide exposure—of this art form paved the way for its idiomatic use. Before the end of the nineteenth century, *song and dance* had developed colloquially for "a rigmarole, an elaborately contrived story or entreaty, a fuss or outcry," according to the *Oxford English Dictionary.*

Within show business, the term also continued to evolve. By the 1920s the phrase had transitioned to describe the lead actor in a musical comedy either in theater or on the big screen. As one would expect, those entertainers were expected to do more than just sing and dance—they also needed to act. This led to another popular expression for the talented performers like Gene Kelly or Shirley Temple who could perform the trifecta: the *triple threat*. Despite Hollywood's embrace of that term, the *triple threat* tag was likely stolen from football, where the phrase became popular beginning in the 1920s to describe a player who could run, kick, and throw the ball.

Stage fright

Anyone who's ever had that dream where you're naked in front of class knows the full power of *stage fright*. Simply put, the term has become a catchall for the fear of any form of performance freak-out.

Not surprisingly, the phrase got its start in the theater. References can be found in newspapers by the 1820s. An 1829 article in the *London Morning Post* described it as "a fatal bar to an aspirant's success" in a story about a new actress in Birmingham, England.

After that, it didn't take long for critics to start explaining what actors felt when gripped with this sort of agony. In 1834 the *London New Monthly Magazine* likened it to "sea-sickness." Over time the effects must have been reassessed as the affliction was upgraded. *Stage fright* could be "perfectly paralysing" to new actors, according to the wonderfully upper-crust-sounding publication *English Gentleman* in 1845.

The term was well known enough by the mid-1800s that it had crossed over to other activities. In an 1865 *Boston Post* story on a top billiards player, a journalist reported, "The 'stage-fright' which had been so perceptible with most of the others on their first essay with the cue, did not appear to bother him in the least."

This outside-the-thespian-world application surely got a big boost in 1876 when one of the era's biggest authors embraced it. Mark Twain picked up the phrase for his classic *The Adventures of Tom Sawyer*. Young Tom is enlisted to recite the "Give me liberty or give me death speech," but a "ghastly stage-fright seized him, his legs quaked under him and he was like to choke." (Twain's description seems a bit more "perfectly paralysing" than "sea sickness.")

Though some modern-day pundits like to use the term *performance anxiety* rather than stage fright (personally, I *never* want to hear *performance anxiety* under any circumstances), stage fright is still a regularly used phrase, and it is a very real threat in both the entertainment industry and elsewhere in the world.

Everyone from Abraham Lincoln to Barbra Streisand has faced it. In fact, according to a 2011 study published in *Backstage* magazine, 84 percent of working actors surveyed admitted to wrestling with this inner demon at least once in their careers.

In terms of handling it, a number of books have been written on the subject, but one 2015 study from the *Journal of Experimental Psychology* goes with the following advice: Get excited about whatever endeavor is making you nervous. Trying to stay calm, the research claims, makes you too introspective about the activity and gets you super-tense.

Stand-in

Stand-in is one of those terms that lost a bit of its Hollywood nuance when it shifted into common conversation.

In the world of TV or movies, a *stand-in* has a very specific role. These professionals literally stand in the place of the actual actor for lighting and preparation purposes before a scene is shot. Generally speaking, a *stand-in* doesn't have to look like the star, but usually the person has some similar attributes like height, skin tone, and hair color. There are even subcategories of *stand-in*s like a "utility stand-in," who can be called upon to replace a number of different actors, or a "number one" stand-in, who is the regular lighting substitute for a production's top star.

While these are demanding jobs (the guy who was the "number one" *stand-in* for Jon Hamm during season four of *Mad Men* worked thirteen or fourteen hours a day, five days a week for six months), you primarily just, well, stand, rather than do the same duties as an

Continued on p. 166

"Why so serious?"
—The Joker (Heath Ledger),
The Dark Knight (2008)

This film line became a worldwide catchphrase before anybody had ever seen the movie. Welcome to the world of twenty-first-century film marketing.

Even after giving it a lot of thought, it's difficult to come up with too many film quotes since 2000 that have become a sustained part of everyday conversation. "I drink your milkshake" from the 2007 film *There Will Be Blood* has its backers, but can you really compare its cultural meaning to the likes of "Frankly my dear, I don't give a damn"? (see p. 12). (*Geek note: There Will Be Blood* writer-director Paul Thomas Anderson took the milkshake idea from the oddest of places—a US senator's testimony on oil-drilling rights, in which he analogized the tasty drink to taking oil during the 1920s Teapot Dome scandal.)

Despite the modern difficulty to break through the clutter, Warner Bros. made sure "Why so serious?" would be different. Beyond anointing it the movie's tagline and circulating posters featuring the line written by the Joker in blood before the film's release, the studio hired a company to set up an alternate-reality game with the phrase at its center. The name of the game was "Why so serious?" and a key element to it required players to go to the website www.whysoserious.com.

In what was a sort of scavenger hunt (often using new media, of course), players sought out clues and swag relating to the Batman film. Overall, some ten million people participated from seventy-five countries. The *Los Angeles Times* called it "one of the most interactive movie-marketing campaigns ever hatched by Hollywood." The effort paid off as *The Dark Knight* was 2008's highest-grossing film.

With that backing and box-office success, the only thing that might have stopped the ubiquity of this expression was tragedy. The "Why So Serious?" posters were already out when, during the film's post-production, Heath Ledger died from an accidental drug overdose. Warner Bros. president and COO Alan Horn immediately went to the actor's family and asked "would you like us to pull this?" Their response was "Heath loved the movie, was very proud of it. This was an accident." So the campaign continued.

It remains a popular meme today and was voted Hollywood's top all-time movie quote by showbiz professionals ages twenty to twenty-nine in a 2016 survey done by the *Hollywood Reporter*. Would the line have enjoyed the same catchphrase longevity if the family had chosen to shut down the marketing? We'll never know, but you can be sure that if a movie wants a piece of dialogue to resonate, this was a really good road map. ★

actor. "You have to have stamina," Jeff Kernaghan, who was Hamm's stand-in, told *Backstage* magazine in 2011. "I was exhausted by the end of the season."

From a language standpoint, a *stand-in* (i.e., a replacement) outside show business is probably more akin to what the movie business calls a *double*. Unlike *a stand-in*, a *double* is expected to look just like the actor he or she might be asked to replace. These players were known to substitute for lazy actors who couldn't be bothered when a director needed to film distant shots. Like a *double*, a non-Hollywood *stand-in* in the board room or on a sports field is supposed to do the same tasks as the person he or she is replacing—only the expectations for performance generally aren't too high.

The term *stand-in* was common-speak on movie sets by at least the 1920s. (There was even a 1937 comedy called *Stand-In*, which featured Joan Blondell in the title role.) The expression was used idiomatically within the next decade.

When it comes to theater, its version of the backup, the *understudy*, became a figure of speech for any sort of standby alternative before the end of the 1800s.

Star

A *star* was born, metaphorically speaking, in the 1700s. The first-known person (thespian or otherwise) to be discussed in print in celestial terms was the legendary British actor David Garrick.

In 1779 a book on theater said: "The little stars, who hid their diminished rays in his [Garrick's] presence, began to abuse him." By all accounts, Garrick deserved praise as the greatest acting light of his generation. "Garrick roused the feelings more than any actor on record . . .," one contemporary proclaimed.

Since then, the number of writers who have used and modified the metaphor has been as plentiful as the real stars in the sky. *To star* (verb) emerged around 1825, and the concept of *stardom* can be found in an O. Henry short story in 1911. The more highly charged *superstar* appears to be an early twentieth-century creation—one that led to the ire of some critics.

"The word 'star' has been used and abused to such an extent that several of the managers are calling their featured players by the more-forced-than-ever word 'super-star,' innocently unmindful of the fun-poking opportunities the ambiguous 'super' part of it affords a merciless punster," an editor at *Photoplay Journal* wrote in 1917.

Even *all-star*, which we now primarily think of as a sports term, got its start in the theater in the latter part of the 1800s. Originally, variety show promoters looking to boost interest in their productions would claim the notoriety and talent of their performers were so grand they were offering an *all-star* show.

Baseball liked the phrase and was quick to pick it up. By the end of the 1880s the term was applied to describe good teams, and the major leagues became the first prominent sports circuit to hold an all-star game in 1933.

With all the hype, Hollywood executives have long griped that many stars become less about producing heat and more about being a gaseous ball. "You make a star, you make a monster," three-time Oscar-winning producer Sam Spiegel said.

Still, it isn't all joy for actors who carry that mantle. Woody Allen expressed that existential angst when a fan once came up to him exclaiming, "You're a star! You're a star." Allen's supposed response: "This year I'm a star, but what will I be next year—a black hole?"

Star-studded

When it comes to infusing big-time celebrity appeal, nobody knows how to do it better than Hollywood's marketing gurus—not even literary luminaries. For generations, great authors have pondered the best way to describe the star-speckled sky. John Milton called it "Star-pav'd" in *Paradise Lost*. Percy Bysshe Shelley dubbed it "Star-inwrought!" in

Continued on p. 170

> ## "You can't handle the truth!"
> ## —Colonel Nathan R. Jessup
> ## (Jack Nicholson),
> ## *A Few Good Men* (1992)

When Jack Nicholson said these words, he wanted to make absolutely sure that everyone on the set knew that they couldn't handle the truth. The climactic scene in which Nicholson's Colonel Nathan R. Jessup character is on the witness stand and is confronted by Lieutenant Daniel Kaffee (Tom Cruise) required a number of different reaction shots.

The speech was a long and emotional one. So when director Rob Reiner completed filming with Nicholson, he told the actor he could go. Reiner knew the speech was tiring and said he'd get someone else to serve as a substitute to read the dialogue while he shot the other actors' responses as they heard the famed "You can't handle the truth!" words.

But Nicholson refused. Even though his additional performances of the speech wouldn't be used in the final cut, he wanted to be the one who delivered the lines. He believed if he did, his fellow cast members would, in return, provide their best reactions.

According to the film's writer, Aaron Sorkin, Nicholson said, "'I just love to act' and he kept doing it all day and all night." The star did forty to fifty takes of the speech, according to one estimate.

Like most writers, Sorkin was pleased with his line's afterlife but is amused by the scope of its pop-culture relevance. On the talk show *Jimmy Kimmel Live!* in 2016, he joked, "I never imagined . . . that Burger King would use it, you know, 'You can't handle this Whopper,' that kind of thing."

While Nicholson's Colonel Jessup made sure (spoiler alert) that everyone knew the truth by the end of the film, one aspect of the movie that was uncertain for a long time was the inspiration for Cruise's character.

Sorkin said that he got the idea for the film from his sister, who as a young military lawyer in the 1980s was actually sent to Guantanamo Bay to try a Marine hazing case. There were a number of defendants and other lawyers on the case, so when the movie hit big, there were at least four attorneys who claimed being the real-life version of Cruise's Kaffee. At least one even made the assertion on his website.

Finally, nearly a decade after the movie's release, Sorkin clarified his motivation—though it's unlikely any of the lawyers happily handled that truth. In a statement through a spokeswoman, Sorkin said, "The character of Dan Kaffee in 'A Few Good Men' is entirely fictional and was not inspired by any particular individual." Needless to say, nobody has tried to take credit for being Nicholson's Jessup. ★

To Night, and H. G. Wells went with "star-dusted sky" in *First Men in the Moon*.

But for all the talents of the aforementioned writers, Hollywood passed on their offerings. Instead, promoters went with *star-studded* to trumpet pictures featuring a cavalcade of renowned actors. The term began popping up in newspaper advertising at the end of the 1920s, but Hollywood went big on this particular sales pitch in 1930.

"Never have you seen such a star-studded carnival of laughs!" crowed a 1930 *Hamilton Daily News* (Ohio) ad for the comedy *Free and Easy*, which was one of many films claiming to be *star-studded* that year. To be fair, the MGM movie did feature such big names as Buster Keaton, Lionel Barrymore, and even the director Cecil B. DeMille. It also bolstered the long-held belief that being *star-studded* can be enough for success, as the picture, which was Keaton's first talking film, was the actor's biggest grossing effort to date despite generally poor reviews.

So why did *star-studded* beat out such contenders as Milton's "star-pav'd" or Shelley's "star-inwrought"? Perhaps it was good ol' patriotism that inspired the Hollywood copywriters to go with an allusion to celestial embroidery. Sure, other writers labeled the night's sky as *star-studded* over the years, but it had been notably deployed to describe the American flag on a number of occasions. No doubt, a subtextual connection to Old Glory would never hurt a movie.

Even if that tie-in did serve as inspiration, the ad men didn't seem to mind that the phrase did show up on occasion in some otherwise very questionable work. Wrote one long-since-forgotten poet named Wm. Nisbet in a 1915 book: "There's a star-studded flag that is dearer to me / Than all the proud banners on earth that I see / Each star means a statehood that can't be undone / And while the flag waves all the states are as one."

Other walks of life—particularly sports—piggybacked on *star-studded* to reflect a top-notch team by the 1950s.

Stay tuned

First instinct might suggest *stay tuned* comes from the musical world. Along those lines, there are examples like a 1916 ad in a Fayetteville, Arkansas, newspaper warning about how lesser brands of pianos just won't "stay tuned." Even metaphorically, there were instances where journalists mined this meaning. In a 1933 *New York Times* story about fears over military buildup in Japan (spoiler alert: the concerns were well founded), a reporter wrote: "Emergencies do not last forever: human nerves do not stay tuned up to the pitch of martial music."

But don't be distracted: There's little doubt that it was radio that delivered *stay tuned* as an idiom. While it may be somewhat forgotten today, back in the primordial days of radio, it was difficult to *stay tuned* thanks to lots of airwave interference (see *bloopers* on p. 20). In fact, when General Electric rolled out a new radio in 1938, it trumpeted its "Keyboard Touch Tuning," which helped make sure that "once tuned they stay tuned to hairline precision."

Aside from that technical element, this phrase, which can be found in conjunction with radio by at least the 1920s, really gained traction in the 1930s when stations used it in advertising to implore listeners to keep listening. For instance, a series of front page *Washington Post* ads in 1938 for WJSV radio used such phrasing as "stay tuned in for the entire broadcast" and "stay tuned for the evening" in selling its programming.

In the same decade, this usage (keeping focused) rather than the musical reference (sounding harmonious) was showing up figuratively as well. In a 1939 *New York Times* report on a speech by US Secretary of Commerce Harry Hopkins, the paper said the key would be to see how President Franklin D. Roosevelt followed up on the cabinet member's statements. "The next thing to do, folks," the paper recommended, "is to tune in on the President—and stay tuned."

Along with *stay tuned*, the need to *tune out* cluttered signals, and *tune in* to the right frequencies in early radio—dating back to their

Continued on p. 174

> "You know how to whistle, don't you, Steve? You just put your lips together and blow."
> —Marie "Slim" Browning (Lauren Bacall), *To Have and Have Not* (1944)

Sometimes a film's dialogue means as much—if not more—to the actors as it does to the audience. That was the case for Lauren Bacall and Humphrey Bogart with these memorable words. The two would fall in love on the set of this film and ultimately marry. Bogart would give Bacall a gold bracelet with a charm whistle on it and, when Bogart died and was cremated in 1957, Bacall would place a small whistle in her husband's urn. It was said to include the inscription, "If you want anything just whistle."

Considering the importance this line had on the couple's relationship, what's remarkable is that they weren't originally written for the movie. Just a teenager in 1943, Bacall had signed a personal contract with powerful director Howard Hawks. Though it took some time, Hawks eventually decided to pair Bacall with Bogart on the film adaptation of Ernest Hemingway's *To Have and Have Not*.

Neither Hemingway's book nor the screenplay, credited to Jules Furthman and William Faulkner, included the dialogue. Instead it was written specifically for Bacall's screen test for the film. Hawks would take credit for writing the scene, saying it "was a scene I wrote as a test for her. I had no idea it was going to be in the picture, but it worked out so well that I wanted to use it." Hawks biographer Todd McCarthy would add that the director's wife at the time, Slim Hawks, believed that she was, at the least, the inspiration for the language from the scene (if not the person who initially stated them in real life). In addition, McCarthy points out that similar language was used in the 1926 film *The Son of the Sheik*, which ends with the line "When I want her, I whistle."

Whatever the starting point, there was no denying Bacall's delivery. She did the screen test with a contract actor named John Ridgely, and though her son Stephen Humphrey Bogart would later write she was embarrassed by all the kissing during rehearsals, she got the role. Hawks was so confident that Bacall could hold her own onscreen with Bogart that he pushed Furthman to add the "whistle scene" to give Bacall the heavyweight dialogue she needed to go toe-to-toe with Bogart.

"You are about the most insolent man on the screen, and I'm going to make the girl a little more insolent than you are," Hawks told Bogart. The actor responded with "fat chance of that" to which Hawks said, "I've got better than fat chance. . . . In every scene you play with her, she's going to walk out and leave you with egg on your face."

This scene, in which Bacall's Marie "Slim" Browning comes on to Bogart's Harry "Steve" Morgan, did just that. ★

original days as a ship-to-ship communication technology in the first decade of the 1900s—also inspired idioms. These terms were being used figuratively by the 1920s (*tuning in* to say you're paying attention and *tuning out* for turning one's thoughts elsewhere).

Tune in got an additional meaning in the 1960s as code for being synchronized with the world (often, it seemed, with the assistance of hallucinogenics). The height of this meaning came in the form of Timothy Leary's famed line "Turn off, tune in, and drop out," which seemed to suggest getting really introspective with a bit of help from LSD.

Even though radio has lost much of its cultural cache over the past handful of decades, and TV shifted from a tuning-necessary analog system to a more precise digital format in 2009, these phrases still survive as nostalgic throwbacks.

Straight out of central casting

While we may quiver nowadays at stereotyping a person as coming *straight out of central casting*, there was a time when that was a really good thing. In the early 1920s, movie star wannabes flocked to Hollywood with dreams of being on the big screen. Many were told that the first way into the biz was as an extra. Knowing this, agents lined up to ferry these hopefuls—there were some thirty thousand people looking for this sort of work in the early 1920s—into nonspeaking background parts.

But the big problem was most of the casting reps were crooked. They skimmed off daily salaries (along with a studio finder's fee, the agents would generally take $1 from an extra's $3-a-day pay). Equally as bad, some of the studio insiders profited off the process as well. One assistant casting director was known to require all prospective male extras to get their pants pressed and laundered at one particular dry cleaner, according to a 1925 *Variety* story. Why? He had an ownership interest in the business.

The studios decided enough was enough and pooled their resources to establish the Central Casting Bureau, which would be the only organization allowed to dole out background actors for all the major filmmakers. As a result, being registered with Central Casting became a possible first step toward Hollywood immortality.

Of course, you did need to fit a certain mold. Broadly, the company provided men and women (and a third category: "handicapped") in four distinct groups—atmosphere, character, specialized, and dress. Though the company might have ferreted out some of the sleaze, it didn't make this a more lucrative line of work. In 1935 the average background player earned a meager $8.97 per week (approximately $155 in today's terms).

Central Casting became a private company in the 1970s and continues to exist, making it even easier than ever to pigeonhole people. Potential extras can be sorted not only by age, height, and hair color but also piercings, freckles, and tattoos. Abilities like juggling, walking on stilts, and even twerking are also duly noted. Apparently, just about anybody can be found on the Central Casting rolls, with two notable exceptions—the Amish and Orthodox Jews, who are apparently very hard to find.

The company became a proxy for a generic example of a type by the 1940s. The syndicated columnist Lucius Beebe wrote in a September 1941 *Washington Post* article that the snooty-looking old folks who sat at window seats in New York's University Club looked "as though they were types sent over from Central Casting specifically for the purpose."

Nevertheless, sometimes having an easily recognizable type of look isn't all bad. Central Casting alums include Brad Pitt and Ava Gardner.

Take a bow

For anybody who has ever had the opportunity to *take a bow* on a stage, it can be an almost religious experience. Historically, there's good reason for that. *Bowing* goes back to ancient times as an act of religious

Continued on p. 178

> ## "You talkin' to me? You talkin' to me? You talkin' to me?"
> ## —Travis Bickle (Robert De Niro), *Taxi Driver* (1976)

Robert De Niro proved in *Taxi Driver* that if you give him a mirror and let him go, he can create an iconic line. In Paul Schrader's script, the only direction in the scene given to his character Travis Bickle was "Travis speaks to the mirror."

"I told Bob [De Niro], 'He's got to say something. He's got to talk to himself,'" director Martin Scorsese said. "We didn't know what. We just started playing with it and that's what came out." De Niro concurred that the development was collaborative. "I'd have an idea about something, talk to Marty about it, try different things," De Niro said in a 1989 interview.

But if you believe a rock legend, the actor had a very clear idea where he got this famous line.

In his 2009 memoir *Big Man: Real Life & Tall Tales*, longtime Bruce Springsteen and the E Street Band saxophonist Clarence Clemons claimed De Niro let him in on the secret inspiration for the actor's improvised dialogue.

De Niro admitted he "stole that" from Springsteen himself, according to the book. Now, Clemons admitted that certain things he included in his memoir were fanciful. But he insisted that while the setting for this tale was fictional, the "story within the story" was "true."

"He did it at a concert," Clemons quoted the actor saying. "At some point he got the whole . . . crowd in a frenzy. Everybody's on their feet screaming their lungs out and saying his name, and he stops in the spotlight and looks out into the howling mass of people and as cool as a . . . cucumber he says, 'Are you talking to me?' Then he looks around to see, to make sure that there's nobody else they could be talking to and he repeats it. 'Are you talking to me? To me? Is that who you're talking to? Are you talking to me?'"

Whether it was the Boss or some other motivation, the line, which has been repeated into countless mirrors across the globe, stood out as a, ahem, mirror into the character's psychotic descent. When De Niro said years later that "there were things that I did in *Taxi Driver* that seemed right," he most surely had that line in mind. ★

obedience. Dead languages like Old English, Old Norse, Old Saxon, Nether-Frankish, and Sanskrit, among others, had a word for this type of submission. (*Geek note*: The English word *bow* comes from the crooked position a person takes in a shape like the weapon we also called a *bow*.)

In the West this act transitioned into the secular world via early European chieftains. They possessed almost godlike respect, so *bowing* to them seemed like the right thing to do. The oldest references in the English language to *bowing*, as in "to incline the body or head . . . in salutation, acknowledgement of courtesy [or] polite assent," can be found in the 1600s, according to the *Oxford English Dictionary*.

Despite the long history of both the action and word, the phrase *take a bow* is fairly new. It didn't begin regularly showing up in US media as part of the theatrical lexicon until the 1880s. It migrated into the language for other entertainers by the start of the 1900s. In 1913 a member of a team of aerial performers told a reporter in Iowa that no matter the level of applause or appreciation, the group would "never 'take a bow' or anything of that sort." When a US boxer fought in front of the king of Italy in 1919, the American ambassador encouraged him to "take a bow" after much adulation. From there the expression became figurative for offering praise beyond public performances.

Nevertheless, it's worth making the observation that you don't always have to do a lot to *take a bow*. In the 1940s a production of *Arsenic and Old Lace* famously paid twelve actors who had not performed in the show to come up and bow at the murder mystery/comedy's conclusion. "For more than a thousand performances, they got howls—as the audience realized they were supposed to be the bodies buried in the cellar," NPR explained in 2012.

Tearjerker

The right formula for a *tearjerker*—those moments when tears can't help but well up in the corners of your eyes and you let out a little sob—apparently depends on the medium.

In theater the syndicated New York columnist O. O. McIntyre, who at one time had a combined circulation of fifteen million readers, described stage actress Paula Lord in 1927 as "America's most finished tear-jerker." Her secret, he said, was "the art of faltering and inarticulate emotionalism."

The film industry had its share of *tearjerkers* as well. Among those noted in one 1955 article were Greta Garbo, Joan Crawford, Norma Shearer, and Loretta Young. The story, which ran in a number of newspapers, dubbed Jane Wyman as the reigning star of the "tear-jerker," which the piece said was also known as a "throat-burner, four-hankie job or, as Jane prefers, the tender love story."

Wyman described the key for big-screen success with this genre as follows: "If I can have women in the audience look at me on the screen and say 'there but for the grace of God go I,' then I'm satisfied." (Alas, she was silent on what leads to sobbing men when watching movies like *The Pride of the Yankees*.)

While the expression started in theater—an early reference can be found in 1912 and spread to the movies by the 1920s—the music business is where the concept has been scientifically tested. According to a study performed by a British psychologist named John Sloboda in the 1990s, a musical feature called an *appoggiatura* is the key. An *appoggiatura* is a type of note that is off the melody just a smidge to create a brief dissonant sound, which is then quickly resolved. The tension, according to the research, can create the emotionally induced eye moisture.

When it comes to real-life *tearjerkers*, which could be found in language outside of the entertainment field by 1940, the secret sauce can vary just as much as their showbiz counterparts. That said, I'm going with a soldier reuniting with his or her family after a tour of duty if you're ever looking to bring on the waterworks.

That's a wrap!

The history of how we got to *that's a wrap* for finishing up a project—movies or otherwise—spans centuries. *Wrap*, as in to cover something or someone up, dates back to the 1300s. From the beginning of its use, the term often inherently included the idea that you were packing up to go somewhere (you may wrap a baby up on a cold night in your house, but usually you'd be wrapping up a package or person to send out the door).

Though it took a while, that understanding trickled into the English language with the phrase *wrap it up* to reflect that time when you should bring a situation, speech, discussion, or event to its completion. T. E. Lawrence (of *Lawrence of Arabia* fame) used it in this fashion in his 1922 work *Seven Pillars*. "The British," he wrote, "were wrapping up the Arabs on all sides—at Aden, at Gaza, at Bagdad."

From there, Hollywood took it. In 1952 the movie *The Bad and the Beautiful* had the actor Walter Pidgeon, who was playing a studio executive, saying, "Wrap it up for the night" to reflect the end of a day's shooting. The actual *that's a wrap* phrase also existed by the 1950s. According to the book *This is Orson Welles*, penned by Welles and Peter Bogdanovich, Charlton Heston wrote in a 1957 journal entry about a day of shooting on the classic film *Touch of Evil*: "At 7:40, Orson said: 'O.K., print. That's a wrap on this set.'"

While this evolution of the phrase appears to track, some in Hollywood have insisted that the term actually comes from a command for what should be done with the physical film after shooting is completed. This claim goes that *wrap* is actually an acronym for "Wind Reel and Process." Set language does have other examples of using these sorts of shortcuts. For instance, *M.O.S.* is a term for filming a scene or shot without sound. (*Geek note*: M.O.S.'s origin is contested. Popular legend is it was an abbreviation for "Mit Out Sound," which early European directors would mistakenly say instead of "without sound," but many other options exist, including "Minus Optical Stripe," "Motor Only Shot," and "Muted on Screen.")

When it comes to transitioning outside of show business, *that's a wrap* appears to have made that move in the 1980s. The *Washington Post* was still defining the "movie" expression for its readers in 1976 and the *Christian Science Monitor* felt it needed to do the same in 1980, calling it "Hollywood language."

Thirtysomething

For baby boomers, nostalgia beats at the heart of this term. The reason: Way back in the late 1980s, the *thirtysomething* expression was started just for them.

It may be hard to remember decades on, but the TV drama *Thirtysomething*, which centered on the lives of young parents from the late baby-boomer generation, was a huge hit. It debuted in 1987 and ran until 1991, winning thirteen Emmy Awards along the way. Conceptually, its title seemed a simple enough statement about people of a certain age. In fact, it existed before the program. Although it appears to be a stray reference, a letter to the editor in a 1981 edition of the *New York Times* described playwright Wendy Wasserstein as a "30-something."

But it was *Thirtysomething* creators Ed Zwick and Marshall Herskovitz who popularized the word with their program's title.

"It wasn't a term," Herskovitz remembered in 2009. "People said things like that, but it wasn't in general use. This was literally the whole conversation: We were writing the pilot, I turned to Ed and I said, 'What should we call this?' and I think it took maybe one second, not two, and Ed said, 'Thirtysomething.' I said 'Oh, okay.' And that was the whole conversation."

When it came to ABC, which aired the series, the execs almost got in the way of this linguistic development. "The network said, 'What does that mean? You can't call it that! We insist that you change it!'" Zwick recalled. To support their position, Herskovitz won the day by quoting the book *Catch-22*. The main character, Zwick said, is asked, "'What kind of a name is Yossarian?' And he says, 'It's Yossarian's name, sir.' That was its name!"

Continued on p. 184

"You're gonna need a bigger boat." —Police Chief Martin Brody (Roy Scheider), *Jaws* (1975)

The building of Jaws—the actual animatronic fish—was a daunting task. One story goes that Walter Cronkite happened to be in Martha's Vineyard during the shooting of the film. When a testing of the shark went terribly wrong, Cronkite joked to director Steven Spielberg, "Have you ever considered a career in broadcasting?"

Ultimately, the crew, which sometimes called the film "Flaws" for all the difficulty it had with the artificial beast, got it going but not without continued problems. The faux shark made a loud noise *"Pu-Pish-Pu-Pish-Pu-Pish,* because it had pistons and air rams driving it" whenever it got going, according to screenwriter Carl Gottlieb. Out in the water, it was also sometimes difficult to coordinate time correctly.

In the scene when Brody (Roy Scheider) sees Jaws for the first time, technicians apparently got the timing wrong. Scheider had just told a joke and the fish wasn't supposed to immediately emerge. But when it prematurely did, Gottlieb said, it startled Scheider, who got up, backed away, and ad-libbed to Quint (Robert Shaw), "you're going to need a bigger boat."

Now, Gottlieb would later retreat on the improvisation claim, saying in a 2013 podcast that he was "confused" about how it came about. And the fact that Scheider also said in 2000 that he couldn't remember if he'd come up with it leaves some doubt about the quote's genesis. Regardless, the writer did say at one point that the filmmakers originally didn't consider it worthy of adding.

"It came right after a laugh line and the timing was impeccable, it was 'joke-beat-terror,'" Gottlieb said in the book *Just When You Thought It Was Safe: A Jaws Companion*. "The audience was coming down off a laugh so when the shark's head appears, it was a perfect accident of timing. It wasn't the selected take of that scene, but when they put it in the movie its perfection only became apparent way after the fact, when the film was being edited. When you took out the cursing of the technicians at the mistake of the shark coming up too soon and the sound of the air, which was a hissing sound, it was very effective."

Despite the enduring acclaim Scheider received for his work on *Jaws*, the actor didn't love that his role in the film tended to overshadow his other great performances. (He was nominated for acting Oscars for both *All That Jazz* and *The French Connection*.) Scheider, who died in 2008, once lamented that his work on *Jaws* would be what's mentioned on his tombstone.

The actor may not have loved *Jaws'* prominence on his résumé, but most everyone else continues to embrace his performance—and line—to this day. Folks from filmmaker Kevin Smith (in the movie *Clerks*) to the creators of a Jeep commercial have referenced the line. In 2015 the *Wall Street Journal* told the story of a shipping company that worked on the dangerous Gulf of Oman. Each time the business got a new order, the company's computer chirped, "You're gonna need a bigger boat!" ★

Even with the show's relatively short run, this moniker resonated quickly, leading to other variations for talking generally about a person's or group's age.

In a 1991 headline, a *Los Angeles Times* article referred to members of Generation X as "twentysomethings." The following year, when Bill Clinton and Al Gore were running together for the White House, they were described as a "fortysomething team." All this led to critical mass with the authoritative *Oxford English Dictionary* adding *thirty-something* (as it's sometimes written today) in 1993. The eminent publication even credited the show for the term's inclusion in its pages.

While *thirtysomething* and the other age-related "somethings" have cemented their place in language, the drama's legacy may be in a bit more of a flux. In 2002 *TV Guide* named *thirtysomething* the nineteenth-best TV show of all time. It still gets love from many today, but in 2013 when the same publication did a list of the "60 Best Series of All Time," *Thirtysomething* wasn't included.

Top banana

Calling a person the *top banana* to reflect his or her great importance—or describing someone as a *second banana* to indicate sidekick status—are pieces of burlesque comedy slang from the first half of the twentieth century.

In 1947 Baltimore's *Sun* gave a rundown of how these odd expressions fit into burlesque lingo.

"The average burlesque company carries three comedians who are always known as First, Second and Third Bananas," the paper explained. "Non-comedians are Straight Men, chorus girls are Slaves, and any female performer who is articulate enough to speak lines has the dignified title of Talking Woman."

While most of that jargon seems pretty straightforward (though the "slaves" bit is clearly very disturbing by today's standards), using a popular fruit as inspiration doesn't quite make sense. While we can't pinpoint the exact banana provenance, there are some theories.

The first is that it was named after a popular prop used by stage comedians of the time. For laughs, the most prominent comedic pro in the troupe would carry around a banana-shaped "bladder club" to smack his lesser colleagues over the head, giving that star the *top banana* status, according to *The Language of American Popular Entertainment*.

An alternative explanation comes from *The Encyclopedia of Vaudeville*, which posits that the term was an analogy to the fact that "the fruit at the top of the stalk is always the ripest and most desirable." Then there's the fact that slipping on a banana peel was a foundational piece of slapstick in comedic theater during this era. It's possible that shtick played into this linguistic creation.

While it was well established in the theater trade, *top banana* may not have been destined for idiom status if not for Phil Silvers. The popular comedian, who once said he "started out as Third Banana at Minsky's," had great fondness for his work in burlesque and in 1951 starred on Broadway in a vehicle for him called *Top Banana*. The musical was a big hit, running 350 performances and spawning a 1954 film of the same name.

This attention surely brought *top* and *second bananas* into the general lexicon. Though, perhaps fitting its station on the stage, being a *third banana* never caught on.

Typecast

Once Hollywood typecasts a performer, it's hard to change that perception.

Consider Ronald Reagan. The B-actor gained enough political clout to run for governor of California in 1966. But when longtime Warner Bros. mogul Jack Warner heard about the development, he just couldn't see the journeyman player in such a leading role and began recasting in his mind.

"No, Jimmy Stewart for governor; Ronald Reagan for best friend," Warner said, according to Reagan, who would go on to win that governor's race before becoming America's fortieth president.

Reagan is just one example of the struggle to overcome being *typecast*. Julie Andrews is another. She had tired enough of the wholesome image she'd developed starring in movies like *The Sound of Music* and *Mary Poppins* that she once put a bumper sticker on her car that said "Mary Poppins is a junkie," poking fun at that persona.

In a 2015 Vulture.com article, a journalist outlined the rationale behind typecasting.

"If they cast somebody who'd never played a cop and it turned out to be a bad choice for whatever reason, they might be blamed," the story explained. "But if they cast somebody who'd played eight cops and it didn't work out this time, they could shrug and say, 'I don't know why he didn't work out—he's played eight cops.'"

Of course, the more positive spin of *typecasting* is being *cast against type*, and that gamble can definitely pay off. Just binge-watch old episodes of *Breaking Bad* if you don't believe me. Some forget that actor Bryan Cranston (Walter White himself) was best known for comedy, having played the goofy dad on the long-running series *Malcolm in the Middle* before getting his signature, Emmy-winning role as a meth kingpin.

Linguistically, the idea of *casting*—as in hiring—an actor in a production dates back to at least the sixteenth century, but casting them to type is a more recent phenomenon. Print references to being *typecast*— or as it was sometimes written, *type-cast* or *type cast*—can be found by the 1920s.

On January 1, 1928, the *New York Times* wrote about a stage actress: "Since New York producers show little inclination to depart from their present system of type casting, Lillian Foster, who is playing the featured role in 'Paradise' at the Forty-eighth Street Theatre, has concluded that she will be an emotional actress the rest of her life."

Continued on p. 189

Well, Isn't That Special? *Saturday Night Live*'s Language Legacy

Ed McMahon's boisterous proclamation, "*Heeeereee's* Johnny," to introduce Johnny Carson on *The Tonight Show* may be TV history's single-most famous late-night statement, but for breadth and depth of memorable late-night lines, *Saturday Night Live* has to be the champ. From the opening "Live from New York, it's *Saturday Night!*" in 1975, the show has dished out multiple generations of water-cooler-worthy quips and expressions.

Kevin Nealon, who was a member of the cast from 1986 to 1995, theorized why *SNL* has enjoyed such a long run as pop-culture dialogue writers. "It seems audiences are like parrots, they like to repeat phrases that either have some kind of cadence to them or are silly," he said in the oral history *Live from New York*. "It's something that everybody can relate to, when they get around at the office Monday morning and just kind of laugh, because everybody kind of recognizes it. They can all be in on the laugh. And they can use it as their own little personal joke."

Here are examples from NBC's long-running not-ready-for-prime-time program:

- "Acting!"—Jon Lovitz (master thespian)
- "And you *aaare*?"—David Spade (Dick Clark's receptionist)
- "*Beisbol* been bery, bery good to me"—Garrett Morris (Chico Escuela)
- "Buh-bye"—David Spade (Total Bastard Airlines)
- "*Daaaaa* Bears"—Various (Bill Swerski's Superfans)
- "I live in a van down by the river"—Chris Farley (Matt Foley)
- "I'm a little verklempt," "Talk amongst yourselves," and "Like *buttah*"—Mike Myers (Linda Richman)

- "I'm Chevy Chase, and you're not"—Chevy Chase (Weekend Update)
- "I'm good enough, I'm smart enough, and doggone it, people like me"—Al Franken (Stuart Smalley)
- "I'm Gumby, dammit!"—Eddie Murphy (Gumby)
- "It's always something"—Gilda Radner (Roseanne Roseannadanna)
- "I've got a fever, and the only prescription is more cowbell"—Christopher Walken (music producer Bruce Dickinson)
- "Jane, you ignorant slut"—Dan Aykroyd (Weekend Update)
- "Makin' copies"—Rob Schneider (The Richmeister)
- "New York's hottest club is . . . this place has everything"—Bill Hader (Stefon)
- "Schwing," ". . . *Not*," and "Party on"—Mike Myers and Dana Carvey (Wayne and Garth of "Wayne's World")
- "Sometimes when I get nervous, I stick my hands under my arms, and then I smell my fingers"—Molly Shannon (Mary Katherine Gallagher)
- "Strategery"—Will Ferrell (George W. Bush)
- "Touch my monkey"—Mike Myers (Dieter from Sprockets)
- "Well, isn't that special?" "How con-veen-ient," and "Could it be . . . Satan?"—Dana Carvey (The Church Lady)
- "We're here to pump you up"—Dana Carvey and Kevin Nealon (Hanz and Franz)
- "We're two wild and crazy guys"—Dan Aykroyd and Steve Martin (The Festrunk Brothers, Yortuk and Georg)
- "Wouldn't be prudent" and "Not gonna do it"—Dana Carvey (George H. W. Bush)
- "Yeah, that's the ticket"—Jon Lovitz (Tommy Flanagan, the pathological liar)
- "You look *mah-velous*" and "It's better to look good than to feel good"—Billy Crystal (Fernando)

As for its broader use, society was employing *typecast* as a synonym for stereotyping by the 1950s. An example: "Right-to-work has been type-cast as a villain in the public mind," the *Wall Street Journal* proclaimed in 1958.

Upstage

When you hear the basics of how the theater technically uses *upstage*, the idiom may seem counterintuitive. Figuratively, *upstaging* means to outshine or show up another. To do so in the theater, one would think you'd be required (to use another straightforward theater idiom) to *take center stage*.

Instead, moving *upstage* means receding to the back of the action. Dating back to at least the 1700s, the pitch of most stages was sloped upward in the back, so if an actor was supposed to move away from the audience, it was called moving *upstage* (or as it was often abbreviated in scripts, *U*).

In view of where *upstagers* are located, how did moving away from the audience become a way to steal attention?

The short answer is *upstaging* is literally a matter of perspective, but I'll hand it over to author Philip Godfrey, who discussed the touchy issue in his 1933 survey of English theater called *Back-Stage*, to provide the finer details.

"'Up-staging' is to take up a position nearer to the back of the scene than the other players," he wrote. "This forces them to turn three-quarter-back to the audience when speaking to the upstage actor, and effectively conceals their facial expression. It is a trick which results in the up-stager attracting more prominence in the scene than he would otherwise have."

Godfrey was no fan of this ham-handed approach and offered a solution to such actions.

"With the chronic up-stager the only remedy for the other actors is to withhold their speech until they have deliberately taken up a position favourable to themselves and, if possible, unfavourable to the offender," he wrote. "This reprisal inevitably slows down the scene, but it also throws the real culprit into unpleasant prominence."

Upstage was being used metaphorically in the first decades of the twentieth century—though, at the time, the meaning wasn't fully set. A 1919 *Washington Post* article used it benignly to reflect being the center of attention in a mention about Centre College. The school's football team had parlayed a combination of victories over Kentucky State and West Virginia along with losses by other schools to make them a team to watch in a strange season. "For all its vagaries it is enough to put Centre very much upstage," the journalist wrote.

But by the 1920s *upstaging* was being used with a bit more of the mischief Godfrey explained in mind. The 1926 movie *Upstage*, starring Norma Shearer, tells the story of a young woman who comes to New York from Bangor, Maine, and lucks into a job on the stage. But as she enjoys success, her ego almost gets in the way of her rise to the top.

Beyond that reference, the word was also used that year in a wire story to describe attention-seeking primates in Springfield, Massachusetts. "Oscar and Agnes, monkeys in the Forest Park Zoo, were a bit upstage today toward the other inmates of the monkey house," the article said.

Wing it

While there are a number of avian-instigated idioms like *coming home on a wing and a prayer* and *winging your way* to your destination, neither *wing it* nor the similarly inspired *waiting in the wings* is among them.

Instead, the wings in question here are those key areas just to the sides of a stage. The basic idea of this preparation space existed back in Roman times. The architect Marcus Vitruvius Pollio, who lived around the dawn of the first millennium, wrote in the fifth book of his opus *De Architectura* that a theater had "projecting wings which afford entrances to the stage, one from the forum, the other from abroad." The English embraced the metaphor in the late 1600s with "wing flat" and then "side-wings" being used, according to author Martin Harrison.

With this context, it's easy to see how *waiting in the wings* got its figurative meaning by at least the 1800s. Just as an actor stands in this location before getting onstage, we all sometimes are *waiting in the wings* (i.e., forestalled before, hopefully, action).

But *winging it*, as in improvising, doesn't immediately compute with our understanding of the *wings*. What does being offstage have to do with making something up on the fly? A couple of slightly different explanations account for this nineteenth-century creation.

The first comes from an 1885 edition of *Stage* magazine. The publication explained that "'To wing' . . . indicates the capacity to play a *rôle* without knowing the text, and the word itself came into use from the fact that the artiste frequently received the assistance of a special prompter, who . . . stood . . . screened . . . by a piece of scenery or a wing." In other words, forgetful or unprepared actors would have people feeding them their lines from the wings.

A variation on that claim came in the 1933 book *Back-stage*. Instead of having human cue cards, actors used the wings to prepare themselves before going on. On occasion, the book said, the actor "must give a performance by 'winging it'—that is, by refreshing his memory for each scene in the wings before he goes on to play it."

Those who made *wing it* a figurative expression probably weren't too bothered by its starting point. As a piece of theater jargon, it was a thoroughly British creation, but Americans made it idiomatic. That happened by the 1950s. As *Esquire* defined it in 1959: "To Wing, to do something without preparation."

NOTES

To make the reading easier, citations for all the quotes in this volume were placed in this section rather than in the body of the text. There are two exceptions: quotes directly from movies and TV are not cited (you should go out and see those productions!) and definitions from the *Oxford English Dictionary* are not included here, unless it wasn't explicit in the text that it came from that work. For further information on those definitions, go to www.OED.com.

Introduction

"You struggle . . . sail through." Paul F. Boller Jr. and Ronald L. Davis, *Hollywood Anecdotes* (New York: William Morrow and Co., 1987), 103.

"Its power . . . serious stuff." "Johnson: What would the doctor prescribe?" *The Economist*, January 30, 2016, 78.

"If music . . . the audio track." Donald Liebenson, "Frankly, my dear, you can quote 'em," *Los Angeles Times*, January 2, 2010, D1.

Ad-libbing

"spoofing, joshing . . . unembroidered kidding." "Not in the Manuscript: The Gentle Art of Kidding and Some of the Better Known Experts at It," *New York Times*, November 21, 1926, X2.

"improvised dialogue." "'Ad-Libbing' for Screen," *New York Times*, October 13, 1929, X5.

"ad libbed . . . 'all Rogers.'" "Ad Lib Stars of Screen a Great Aid to Authors," *Washington Post*, September 29, 1929, A2.

Audition

"applied for an audition." "En-Passant," *The Theatre*, August 1, 1879, 36.

"There isn't . . . the world." Peter Hay, *Movie Anecdotes* (New York: Oxford University Press, 1990), 3.

"I didn't . . . go in there." Carl Fussman, "10th Anniversary: What I've Learned," *Vanity Fair*, January 1, 2008, 96.

"All right Mr. DeMille, I'm ready for my close-up"

"harassed head . . . Pomona [California]," "fantastic stamina," and "a woman . . . effects whatever." Anthony Slide (editor), *"It's the Pictures That Got Small" Charles Brackett on Billy Wilder and Hollywood's Golden Age* (New York: Columbia University Press, 2015), 348, 378, 378.

"When he consulted . . . back in the movies." Gene Phillips, *Some Like It Wilder: The Life and Controversial Films of Billy Wilder* (Lexington, Kentucky: The University Press of Kentucky, 2010), 110.

"God forgive . . . Mae West." Philip Gourevitch (introduction), *The Paris Review Interviews: Vol. 1* (New York: Picador, 2006), 419.

"from Mae's . . . camera shot." Sam Staggs, *Close-Up on Sunset Boulevard: Billy Wilder, Norma Desmond and the Dark Hollywood Dream* (New York: St. Martin's Press, 2002), 9.

Backdrop

"manager fell . . . back-drop." "The Understudy," *The Leader* (Kackley, Kansas), September 14, 1893, 1.

"Stores, old . . . lower bay." "Dewey Welcomed in New York," *Salt Lake City Tribune*, September 30, 1899, 1.

"scene painters." "Notes of the Stage," *New York Times*, August 30, 1891, 13.

Backstory

"themselves up . . . mere prologue." Francis X. Clines, "About New York: 'Ryan's Hope' Is a New Yorker's Fantasy," *New York Times*, November 27, 1976, 15.

"back story . . . good community." Robert M. Franklin, "Faith and poverty; Rediscovering the Back Story of Christmas," *New Pittsburgh Courier*, January 4, 2006, B2.

"What we . . . the piece" and "We at . . . the phrase." William Safire, "back story," *New York Times*, August 7, 2005, 6.16.

"both a . . . back story." Richard Cohen, "Obama's Back Story," *Washington Post*, March 27, 2007, A13.

"Fasten your seat belts, it's going to be a bumpy night."

"Those are . . . more venom." Sam Staggs, *All About All About Eve: The Complete Behind-the-Scenes Story of the Bitchiest Film Ever Made* (New York: St. Martin's Griffin, 2000), 138.

"darling" and "hoisting storm warnings." Mel Gussow, "Film: The Lasting Allure of 'All About Eve,'" *New York Times*, October 1, 2000, 2.13.

"The line . . . man's cliché." Vincent Canby, "Critic's Notebook: 40 Years of Film Magic," *New York Times*, November 20, 1992, C1.

Behind the scenes

"Nearly all . . . curtain is up." Olive Logan, "The Secret Regions of the Stage," *Harper's New Monthly Magazine*, April 1874, 628.

"But there . . . the Scenes." John Dryden, *Dramatik Works, Volume 1* (London: J. Tonson, 1735), lviii.

"Many Noblemen . . . the Play." "Advertisements," *The Post Boy* (London), February 4, 1701, 2.

"Our handling . . . the scenes." Kerry O'Brien "Roxon defends stance on private health insurance tax," December 5, 2008, http://www.abc.net.au/7.30/con tent/2007/s2242541.htm.

big picture, The

"big picture." "At the Theater," *East Liverpool Evening News* (Ohio), February 11, 1904, 4.

"The vaudeville . . . o'clock sharp." "Five Vaudeville Thrillers and All Stars at Parras—'The Cowardly Way Is Big Picture Opening Today's Bill," *Bakersfield Californian*, January 5, 1916, 7.

"When I first . . . a lie!'" Peter Hay, *Movie Anecdotes* (New York: Oxford University Press, 1990), 54.

Frankly my dear, I don't give a damn.

"The omission . . . an American Bible." Steve Wilson, *The Making of Gone with the Wind* (Austin: University of Texas Press, 2014), 320.

"a very stormy session." Aljean Harmetz, *On the Road to Tara: The Making of Gone with the Wind"* (New York: Harry N. Abrams, 1996), 147.

"essential and . . . good nature." Jon Lewis, *Hollywood v. Hard Core: How the Struggle over Censorship Saved the Modern Film Industry* (New York: New York University Press), Location 7139 (Kindle version).

Bit part

"bit part." "For Taking Small Part, Actor Gets Fat Role in New Film," *Dunkirk* (New York) *Evening Observer*, November 21, 1925, 16.

"Politicians don't . . . the opera," "Paul Ryan, as speaker of the House." *Washington Times*, October 21, 2015, http://www.washingtontimes.com/news/2015/oct/21/editorial-paul-ryan-as-speaker-of-the-house/.

Blackout

"Is the mere . . . as these? "Stagecraft of 'The Ring,'" *The Times* (London), May 19, 1928, 12.

Goldwynisms

"to the general . . . word manglings." Albin Krebs, "Samuel Goldwyn Dies at 91," *New York Times*, February 1, 1974, 34.

"It sounds . . . on Sam." *Oxford English Dictionary* (*Goldwynism* entry), www.OED.com.

"Goldwynisms weren't . . . press agents." "Real Goldwynisms stand out," *Sun* (Baltimore), February 19, 1974, B4.

Blockbuster
"destined . . . box-office blockbuster!" "Random House Books" (advertisement), *New York Times*, April 2, 1944, BR16.

Bloopers
"a person . . . his neighbors" and "overcome this . . . and patience." "Don't Be a Blooper," *Wisconsin Rapids Daily Tribune*, December 2, 1924, 8.

"has made . . . in town" and "the 'blooper' . . . sudden death." "There's a Radio 'Blooper' Here Seeking Trouble," *Sumner* (Iowa) *Gazette*, February 25, 1926, 1.

"help yourself . . . for you." "Bloopers! Clear the Air! Get Rid of the Squealers!" (advertisement), *Chester* (Pennsylvania) *Times*, May 26, 1926, 3.

"To forgive . . . err, divine." Kermit Schafer, *Prize Bloopers* (New York: Avenel Books, 1979).

"Go ahead, make my day"
"No matter . . . my day." Ronald Reagan, "American Business Conference: Remarks at a meeting with business executives," *Public Papers of Presidents*, March 13, 1985, 295.

"Some New . . . Is Needed." "Some New Material Is Needed," March 16, 1985, A20.

"If you . . . good enough," "Once a method . . . You decide," and "I'll be honest . . . squint." Donald Liebenson, "Frankly, my dear, you can quote 'em," *Los Angeles Times*, January 2, 2010, D1.

"I knew . . . chill night . . ." Robert Hendrickson, *The Facts on File Encyclopedia of Word and Phrase Origins* (Fourth Edition), (New York: Checkmark Books, 2008), 531.

Bogart
"muscle through." *Oxford English Dictionary* (*Bogart* entry), www.OED.com.

Bombshell
"A Bombshell . . . starlet potential," "Every movement . . . a chair," and "The Bombshell . . . tradition." Laren Stover and Kimberly Forrest, *The Bombshell Manual of Style* (New York: Hyperion, 1997), 18, 20, 43.

"Here's looking at you, kid"

"the incident . . . invented" and "Luis [sic] . . . beautiful friendship." Aljean Harmetz, *The Making of Casablanca: Bogart, Bergman, and World War II* (New York: Hyperion, 1992), 187, 263.

Bringing down the house

"It is . . . hearty applause." "The Pilgrim Fathers." *Flag of Our Union*, October 7, 1854, 317.

"It is . . . grotesque sayings." "Harlequin vs. Dryasdust," *New York Evangelist*, February 20, 1879, 4.

"Houston, we have a problem"

"Okay, Houston . . . problem here" and "Houston . . . a problem." National Aeronautics and Space Administration, *Apollo 13 Technical Air-to-Ground Voice Transcription*, 160.

"You know . . . correct tense." Tom Hanks, "The 10th anniversary edition of 'Apollo 13' released on DVD today," *Today*, March 29, 2005, 7 a.m.

"The line . . . true story." Janet Maslin, "'Apollo 13,' a Movie for the Fourth of July," *New York Times*, June 30, 1995, C1.

Cast of thousands

"My God . . . the war." Paul F. Boller Jr. and Ronald L. Davis, *Hollywood Anecdotes* (New York: William Morrow and Co., 1987), 402–403.

"a cast . . . of people." "To Produce 'Cabiria' Here," *Loredo Times* (Texas), January 16, 1916, 9.

"a cast . . . every State." Rosamond Pinchot Aids the Smith Campaign; Nun of 'Miracle' Tests Speakers' Abilities," *New York Times*, August 29, 1928, 4.

Catcall

"The cat-call . . . of nonsense . . ." and "The cat-call . . . into fits." Joseph Addison, *The Works of the Right Honourable Joseph Addison, Esq.; Volume the Third* (London: Jacob Tonson, 1721), 74.

"the horrible . . . the catcall." "July, 1834: Original Communications," *Magazine of Natural History, and Journal of Zoology, Botany, Mineralogy, Geology and Meteorology* (London: Longman, Rees, Orme, Brown, Green and Longman, 1834), 289.

Cattle call

"Actors are Cattle" and "I have . . . treated as cattle." Peter Hay, *Movie Anecdotes* (New York: Oxford University Press, 1990), 60.

"Just another . . . accurate one." Bill Slocum, "Pulchritude Aplenty: Another 'Cattle Call,'" *San Antonio Light* (Texas), June 19, 1961, 17.

"The airline . . . road warriors." Scott McCartney, "The Middle Seat: Unusual Route: Discount Airlines Woo Business Set," *Wall Street Journal*, February 19, 2008, http://www.wsj.com/articles/SB120338017328875635.

Cleavage

"The Mason . . . political cleavage." "Texas (continued from page 1)," *Amarillo Sunday News and Globe* (Texas), May 18, 1930, 18.

"the shadowed . . . distinct sections." *Oxford English Dictionary* (*Cleavage* entry), www.OED.com.

"rather nice." "Wicked but Nice," *Times* (London), April 18, 1983, 12.

"cleavage." Bob Thomas, "After Jaunt to Broadway," *Medicine Hat Daily News* (Canada), May 14, 1948, 8.

"I coulda been a contender"

"Well, I was . . . in my mind." T. J. Quinn, "Wonderful Life. The 'Golden Boy,' Roger Donoghue, was a true inspiration," *New York Daily News*, August 27, 2006, http://www.nydailynews.com/archives/sports/wonderful-life-golden -boy-roger-donoghue-true-inspiration-article-1.655556.

"Whether it's . . . the world." Abby Ellin, "I Coulda Been a Contender," *Psychology Today*, July 1, 2010, https://www.psychologytoday.com/articles/201007/ i-coulda-been-contender.

"Cliffhanger"

"Was Death . . . his hand?" Thomas Hardy, "Chapter XXII 'Love Will Find Out the Way,'" *Tinsley's Magazine*, March 1873, 122.

"cliffhanger." "Serial Loses Lead," *Variety*, June 16, 1931.

"'Cliffhanger' Interactive . . . the Gridlock." Azmat Khan, "'Cliffhanger' Inter-active: A Guide to the Gridlock," PBS.org, February 13, 2013, http://www.pbs.org/ wgbh/pages/frontline/government-elections-politics/cliffhanger/cliffhanger-inter active-a-guide-to-the-gridlock/.

Cloak-and-dagger

"Those who . . . the heart." "Speech falsely attributed to Earl C—m," *Gentle-man's Magazine*, July 1769, 343.

"I love the smell of napalm in the morning"

"That scene . . . room [floor]." Andrew Edwards, "'Apocalypse Now' writer journeys into the heart of Cal State San Bernardino," *San Bernardino Sun* (Califor-nia), November 6, 2008, NEWS.

"like waving . . . a bull." Joey Figueroa, Zak Knutson (directors), *Milius* (documentary), 2013.

Close-up

"We paid . . . of him," "Museums are . . . liver and lungs," and "What are . . . for the exits!" Peter Hay, *Movie Anecdotes* (New York: Oxford University Press, 1990), 4.

"Properly speaking . . . the scene." Epes Winthrop Sargent, *Technique of the Photoplay* (Second Edition) (New York: The Moving Picture World, 1913), 16.

"Collect as . . . to overdose." Tony Bill, *Movie Speak: How to Talk Like You Belong on a Film Set* (New York: Workman, 2008), 40.

Cue

"a slip . . . the tongue." *Oxford English Dictionary* (*Miscue* entry), www .OED.com.

"I see dead people"

"I see dead people," "And then . . . voices came," and "the voices . . . it back." Michael Bamberger, *The Man Who Heard Voices or, How M. Night Shyamalan Risked His Career on a Fairy Tale* (New York: Gotham Books, 2006), 10.

"It just . . . big break" and "When we . . . the story." Daniel Hajek, "Before 'I See Dead People,' Haley Joel Osment Saw Casting Agents at Ikea," NPR, July 13, 2015, http://www.npr.org/2015/07/12/422317464/a-career-spanning-two-decades -began-at-ikea.

Curtains (the curtain falls)

"When the . . . is ready." Olive Schreiner, *The Story of an African Farm: A Novel*" (Boston: Roberts Brothers, 1883), 8.

"Ah! The tale . . . curtain falls." "Reflections on the Life and Death of Lord Clive," *Pennsylvania Magazine*, March 1775, 107.

"It's curtains . . . Bob Fitzsimmons." "Lanky Bob Loses a Mill in Twelve Rounds," *The Fort Wayne Sentinel* (Indiana), December 29, 1909, 4.

Cut to the chase

"Jannings escapes . . . to chase" and "I am . . . instructions later." *Oxford English Dictionary* (*Cut* entry), www.OED.com.

"When in . . . the chase." Frederick C. Othman, "In Hollywood: Helen Deutsch Has Mottos for Successful Authorship," *Winnipeg Free Press* (Canada), March 10, 1944, 4.

"3 basic . . . Good Enough.'" Leonard Lyons, "The Lyons Den," *Amarillo Sunday News-Globe* (Texas), March 13, 1949.

I'll Have Two Movie Stars Straight Up: Drinks with Star Appeal

"Italian vermouth . . . [and] gin." Hubbard Keavy, "Screen Life in Hollywood," *Register* (Sandusky, Ohio), September 5, 1934, 9.

"French vermouth." E. V. Durling, "On the Side," *Era* (Bradford, Pennsylvania), November 18, 1955, 12.

Don't touch that dial

"Don't touch . . . new one." Ruth Walker, "Don't touch that dial!" *Christian Science Monitor*, July 14, 2006, 18.

"Some investors . . . that dial." "The New Year Brings New Opportunities for Investors," *Washington Post*, January 7, 2013, A22.

"Don't Touch . . . Meager's Market," Meager's Market (advertisement), *Syracuse Herald-Journal* (New York), August 20, 1941, 13.

Double take

"most sudden reaction . . . other performer" and "a somewhat . . . should be." Don B. Wilmeth, *The Language of American Popular Entertainment* (Westport, Connecticut: Greenwood Press, 1981), 267.

"the old . . . Sennett vintage." "Alice Brady Does Old Comedy Gags," *Washington Post*, August 13, 1937, 12.

"There are . . . as many as 20." United Press International, "Comedy Crowd Has a Lingo of Cryptic Import," *Washington Post*, June 5, 1936, X13.

"If you build it, he will come"

"told that . . . Ed Harris." W. P. Kinsella, "Where it began: 'Shoeless Joe,'" ESPN.com, April 21, 2014, http://espn.go.com/mlb/story/_/id/10797026/mlb-wp-kinsella-25th-anniversary-field-dreams.

"What happened . . . feet tall" and "You have . . . very selfish." Christian Red, "Field of Dreams: 25 years ago, a film about a disgraced ballplayer, a magical cornfield & fathers and sons became an American masterpiece," *New York Daily News*, April 26, 2014, http://www.nydailynews.com/sports/baseball/zone-25-years-field-dreams-american-masterpiece-article-1.1769876.

"old saying." Kathie Lee Gifford, "Hoda and Kathie Lee discuss current events," *Today* (NBC News Transcripts), February 19, 2009, 7 a.m.

Drama queen

"If he is . . . a failure," Richardson Wright, "Father Is Placated by Having Room to Pursue His Hobbies," *Washington Post*, December 10, 1923, 14.

"Academy drama queen." "The Emperor's Candlesticks" (advertisement), *Monitor-Index and Democrat* (Moberly, Missouri), November 11, 1937, 12.

"a majorette . . . drama queen." Louella O. Parsons, "Hollywood," *Anderson Daily Bulletin* (Indiana), December 8, 1955, 17.

"daytime drama . . . dead mackerel.'" "T.V. Schedule," *Tyrone Daily Herald* (Pennsylvania), October 29, 1973, 7.

"He's a drama . . . the spotlight." FoxSports.com, "Jimmy Johnson: Favre's a 'drama queen,'" *La Prensa* (San Antonio, Texas), October 17, 2010, 1B.

Dress rehearsal

"Will [the critic] . . . 'dress rehearsal'?" Untitled, *New York Daily Times*, September 29, 1852, 4.

"A dress rehearsal." "A dress rehearsal," *Mr. Punch's Victorian Era*, September 12, 1868, 173.

"A dress rehearsal . . . with spirit." "Helena Modjeska," *Temple Bar: A London Magazine for Town and Country Readers*, January 1883, 85.

"The dress rehearsal . . . and manager." Arthur Hornblow, "How a play is produced," *Frank Leslie's Popular Monthly*, November 1893, 622.

"I'll be back"

"the biggest disagreement," "I felt . . . rugged to me," "The truth . . . understand contractions," and "I will . . . to write." Arnold Schwarzenegger with Pete Petre, *Total Recall: My Unbelievably True Life Story* (New York: Simon & Schuster, 2012), 313.

Fade-out

"trick pictures," "It was not . . . characters involved," and "Experimenting only . . . her lover." Homer Croy, *How Motion Pictures Are Made* (New York: Harper & Brothers, 1918), 153, 153, 176.

"The veriest . . . 'fade-out' of love." *Punch, or the London Charivari*, March 21, 1928, 318.

"I'm as mad as hell and I'm not going to take this anymore"

"unfair," "bitterness," "hatchet job," "To me . . . take offense," "rather amusing," and "pretty funny." Tom Shales, "'Network': Hating TV Can Be Fun," *Washington Post*, October 24, 1976, H1.

"Between the . . . any more,'" "There are . . . the one," and "Well, I'm . . . could finish." David Itzkoff, *Mad as Hell: The Making of Network and the Fateful Vision of the Angriest Man in Movies* (New York: Times Books, 2014), 110, 179, 179.

Gaslight

"It is . . . mental illness." *Oxford English Dictionary* (*Gaslight, v.,* entry), www
.OED.com.

"Mister . . . of Dodge." Jack Smith, "Great Moments in . . . History Are Hol-
low," *Amarillo Daily News* (Texas), March 14, 1960, 8.

"Get out . . . Ma'am." United Press International, "Get Out of Dodge,
Ma'am," *Las Vegas Sun*, 21.

"lay low." "How They Communicate," *The Telegraph-Herald* (Dubuque,
Iowa), May 16, 1965, 14.

"White tricks . . . of Dodge." Chauncey Bailey, "Vice Cop: Another 'Trick' on
Black Folks," *Sun Reporter* (San Francisco), March 31, 1973, 10.

Get the hook

"an impossible . . . tenor voice," "With this . . . had happened," "worst imaginable," and "Get the hook!" "'Get the Hook' Was Coined by a New York Gallery
God," *Milford* (Iowa) *Mail*, September 24, 1908, 3.

"bedlam broke loose" and "Get the . . . hook!" "Playhorse with Hanly," *Rock-
port Democrat* (Indiana), June 26, 1908, 1.

Going off-script

"The story . . . from the story." Homer Croy, *How Motion Pictures Are Made*
(New York: Harper & Brothers, 1918), 104.

"'Script,' in . . . newspaperman's 'copy.'" Albert Parry, "Movie Talk," *American
Speech*, June 1928, 365.

"the screen play . . . year." Romeo and Juliet (advertisement), *Evening Democrat* (Fort Madison, Iowa), December 1, 1916, 4.

"I'm going to make him an offer he can't refuse"

"I wrote . . . money" and "He rewrote . . . a director." Mario Puzo, *The Godfather Papers* (excerpted in *The Making of the Godfather*) (New York: G.P. Putnam's
Sons, 1972), Locations 66, 445 (Kindle version of *The Making of the Godfather*).

"The [Robards] . . . was benevolent." "Make him an offer he can't refuse," The
Phrase Finder, http://www.phrases.org.uk/meanings/an-offer-he-cant-refuse.html.

"I'd always . . . it better." Charles McGrath, "Revisiting a Potboiler You Can't
Improve?" *New York Times*, November 16, 2004, E1.

Groundhog Day

"The first . . . falling together." "Big Think Interview with Danny Rubin,"
www.bigthink.com, 2014, http://bigthink.com/videos/big-think-interview-with
-danny-rubin.

"I think . . . 30 or 40 years." "Harold Ramis Responds to Wolf Gnards," www.wolfgnards.com, http://www.wolfgnards.com/index.php/2009/08/18/harold-ramis-responds-to-the-wolf-gnards.

"I'm the king of the world!"

"a dynamic document" and "the bones . . . can yield." James Cameron (foreword), *James Cameron's Titanic*, (New York: Harper Perennial, 1997), 9.

"Jim even . . . moved on." E-mail correspondence between author and Jon Landau, January 27, 2016.

"I took . . . of triumph." Director's commentary, *Special Collector's Edition: Titanic* (2005).

"Titanic Alert" and "off the extreme . . . vessel." Stephen J. Spignesi, *The Titanic for Dummies* (Hoboken, New Jersey: John Wiley & Sons, 2012), 320.

Ham (hamming it up)

"exaggerated movements . . . their act." Don B. Wilmeth, *The Language of American Popular Entertainment* (Westport, Connecticut: Greenwood Press, 1981), 123.

"a ham. Regular hamfatter." "Brilliant," *Oak Park Reporter* (Illinois), January 25, 1889, 6.

Hollywood ending

"How can . . . the level?" Paul F. Boller Jr. and Ronald L. Davis, *Hollywood Anecdotes* (New York: William Morrow and Co., 1987), 363.

"where they . . . the living" and "where you . . . cold shoulders." Peter Hay, *Movie Anecdotes* (New York: Oxford University Press, 1990), 199.

"Anywhere you . . . in jeopardy." Frank S. Nugent, "Mr. Ruggles Has the Word for It," *New York Times*, October 25, 1936, X5.

"It's alive, it's alive!"

"The adaptation . . . this screenplay," "'Frankenstein': Read THR's 1931 Review," *Hollywood Reporter*, November 15, 2014, NEWS.

"The wrath . . . his reveries." Marjorie Driscoll, "Had to Flee His Frankensteins," *Salt Lake Tribune* (Utah), March 7, 1937, 4.

In sync

"The talking . . . these words." Epes Winthrop Sargent, *Technique of the Photoplay* (Second Edition) (New York: The Moving Picture World, 1913), 127.

"Synchrony between . . . to attain." Homer Croy, *How Motion Pictures Are Made* (New York: Harper & Brothers, 1918), 301.

In the limelight

"really threw . . . glittering fairyland." Allardyce Nicoll, *History of English Drama, 1660–1900* (Cambridge, England: Cambridge University Press, 1962), 46.

"We need . . . the limelight." Calvin Coolidge, *Have Faith in Massachusetts* (Boston: Houghton Mifflin Co., 1919), 46.

Lights! Camera! Takeoff? Movie Glitz at Airports

"I think . . . Farrah-Fawcett-Majors Airport." United Press International, "'John Wayne Airport' in Los Angeles?" *Elyria Chronicle* (Ohio), March 13, 1979, A5.

"Wouldn't it be . . . John Wayne." Caitlin Liu, "'Bob Hope Airport' Could Land in Burbank," *Los Angeles Times*, November 4, 2003, B4.

"legal name." Anthony Clark Carpio, "Bob Hope Airport will be branded 'Hollywood Burbank Airport,'" *Los Angeles Times*, May 3, 2016, http://www.latimes.com/local/lanow/la-me-ln-bob-hope-airport-hollywood-20160503-story.html.

It's showtime!

"The dresses . . . is exhibited." Edmund Burke, "Letters on a Regicide Peace," *The Works of Edmund Burke*, Volume 5 (London: George Bell & Sons, 1903), 337.

"truly a sad . . . go on." *The Democrat* (Fort Wayne, Indiana), October 8, 1870, 8.

"It's Show-time again." Budd-Michelin (advertisement), *Life*, January 28, 1926, 3.

Jump the shark

"All successful . . . six seasons?" and "I likened . . . was laugh." Fred Fox Jr., "First Person: In defense of 'Happy Days' 'Jump the Shark' episode," *Los Angeles Times*, September 3, 2010, http://articles.latimes.com/2010/sep/03/entertainment/la-et-jump-the-shark-20100903.

"May the force be with you"

"there must . . . force, reality," "The 'Force . . . call it," "May the Lord . . . spirit" and "May the force of others . . . you." J. W. Rinzler, *The Making of Star Wars* (New York: Ballantine Books, 2007), Locations 840, 844, 847 878 (Kindle version).

"an echo." Steve Silberman, "Life After Darth," www.wired.com, May 1, 2005, http://www.wired.com/2005/05/lucas-2/?pg=3.

"The message . . . us all." "Star Wars Day: May the Fourth Be with You," www.starwars.com, http://www.starwars.com/may-the-4th.

Keystone Cops

"a quick-thinking . . . he owed" and "Sennett . . . working class." Brent E. Walker, *Mack Sennett's Fun Factory* (Jefferson, North Carolina: McFarland & Co., 2010), 25, 28.

"if it was . . . enough for us." Ezra Goodman, "Mack Sennett and the Lost Art of Slapstick," *New York Times*, February 15, 1948, X5.

"Maybe people . . . in grammar." Murray Schumach, "Sennett Decries Modern Comedy," *New York Times*, April 20, 1959, 36.

Lay an egg

"Wall St. . . . an Egg." "Wall St. Lays an Egg," *Variety*, October 30, 1929, 1.

"laid enough . . . Armenians." "Mutt and Jeff," *Variety*, October 18, 1926, 41.

"in the inelegant . . . this season." David J. Walsh, "Second Baseman Needed By Giants," *Telegraph-Herald and Times-Journal* (Dubuque, Iowa), April 7, 1929, 16.

"My momma always said, 'Life was like a box of chocolates. You never know what you're gonna get'"

"Groom . . . than this." "Forrest Gump," *Publishers Weekly*, http://www.publishersweekly.com/978-0-385-23134-3.

"I tried to . . . stupid does'" and "Upon going . . . going to get." Donald Liebenson, "Frankly, my dear, you can quote 'em," *Los Angeles Times*, January 2, 2010, D1.

"Let me say . . . you shabby." Winston Groom, *Forrest Gump* (New York: Vintage Books, 1986), 1.

"took the . . . character." William Grimes, "Following the Star of a Winsome Idiot," *New York Times*, September 1, 1994, http://www.nytimes.com/1994/09/01/movies/following-the-star-of-a-winsome-idiot.html?pagewanted=all.

Leading Role

"The term . . . (as into battle)." Martin Harrison, *The Language of Theatre* (New York: Routledge, 1998), 139.

"navigation's leading . . . light." William Safire, "On Language: No Leading Role," *New York Times*, December 17, 1989, A16.

Looney Tunes

"If Walt . . . vindictive guy." E-mail correspondence between author and J. B. Kaufman, January 25, 2016.

"A group . . . 'Looney Tunes.'" "A Few of the Intricacies Involved in a Looney Tune," *Washington Post*, April 5, 1931, A4.

"We are . . . Third Reich." United Press International, "Reagan Blasts Terrorist States," *Chicago Tribune*, July 9, 1985, http://articles.chicagotribune.com/1985-07 -09/news/8502140217_1_squalid-criminals-strangest-collection-fanatical-hatred.

"Roads? Where we're going, we don't need roads."

"Never has . . . need roads.'" Ronald Reagan: "Address Before a Joint Session of Congress on the State of the Union ," February 4, 1986. Online by Gerhard Peters and John T. Woolley, *The American Presidency Project*. http://www.presidency.ucsb .edu/ws/?pid=36646.

"It was one . . . breath here," "it was . . . coincidence," "We always . . . different ways," "want to see . . . different," and "This was . . . a submarine." Telephone interview between author and Bob Gale, March 22, 2016.

Marquee

"in a . . . the purpose." "The Chrysanthemum Show," *New York Times*, November 9, 1888, 8.

"in the marquee . . . camp." "A Breakfast in Honor of Simon Cameron," *Washington Post*, August 10, 1887, 1.

"an elaborate . . . bronze." "40th Season at Ford's," *Sun* (Baltimore, Maryland), September 5, 1911, 9.

Melodramatic

"Melodrame Man!" "The taste . . . intellectual powers," and "melodramatic mode." Elaine Hadley, *Melodramatic Tactics: Theatricalized Dissent in the English Marketplace, 1800–1885* (Stanford, California: Stanford University Press, 1995), 1, 2–3, 1.

They're *G-r-r-r-eat*: TV Commercials

"I've always . . . around it." Mary Kaye Schilling, "Jason Bateman, Act Two," *New York Magazine*, August 23, 2010.

Mickey Mouse

"the best-known . . . dark hour." L. H. Robbins, "Mickey Mouse Emerges as Economist," *New York Times*, March 10, 1935. SM8.

"self-respecting . . . 'mickey-mouse music.'" And "Where the . . . emotional depth!" George T. Simon, "The Big Bands—Count Basie and Sammy Kaye," *Daily Democrat* (Woodland, California), January 16, 1968, 13.

"Who doesn't . . . 'Mickey Mouse'?" and "If sailors are ordered to slap . . . at persona expense, that is Mickey Mouse." Elmo R. Zumwalt Jr., ". . . on the Navy," *New York Times*, December 3, 1977, 23.

"I only hope . . . by a mouse." Fred R. Shapiro (editor), *The Yale Book of Quotations* (New Haven, Connecticut: Yale University Press, 2006), 206.

Miscast

". . . people crowd . . . the same." "Howard's Letter," *Boston Sunday Globe*, February 26, 1888, 9.

"I had heretofore . . . to play," Elizabeth Phipps Train, *Madam of the Ivies* (Philadelphia: J. B. Lippincott Co., 1898), 30.

"Say hello to my little friend!"

"more commonly . . . leetle *fren*'!" and "It was like . . . it works." Ken Tucker, *Scarface Nation: The Ultimate Gangster Movie and How It Changed America*" (New York: St. Martin's Griffin, 2008), Locations 754, 828 (Kindle version).

"catchy phrase" and "Oliver Stone . . . of Oliver." Al Pacino, "Rare & Revealing Interview with Al Pacino," *CNN: Larry King Live*, December 17, 2010, 9 p.m.

"You can never . . . nobody noticed." B. J. Sigesmund, "The Return of Greed," *Newsweek*, July 19, 2002, Arts and Entertainment.

Mob scene

"The Great Mob Scene." Front Street Theatre (advertisement), *Sun* (Baltimore, Maryland), November 5, 1862, 2.

"The production . . . the ensemble." "A Man's Man," *Motion Picture News*, January 6, 1912, 7.

"Mob scene . . . the director." Peter Milne, *Motion Picture Directing: The Facts and Theories of the Newest Art* (New York: Falk Publishing Co., 1922), 88.

Money shot

"'the money shot' . . . its expense." Linda Williams, *Hard Core: Power, Pleasure, and the 'Frenzy of the Visible'* (Berkeley, California: University of California Press, 1989), 93.

"Bobby Jones . . . a money shot." *Oxford English Dictionary* (*Money shot* entry), www.OED.com.

"Wonder if . . . money shot?" Maury White, "Maury White," *Des Moines Register* (Iowa), October 28, 1969, 1S.

"Show me the money!"

"I said, basically . . . the money." Mal Florence, "Now He Should Say, 'Show Me the Residuals!'" *Los Angeles Times*, May 25, 1997, http://articles.latimes.com/1997-05-25/sports/sp-62509_1_jerry-maguire.

"He was actually . . . the money." Lea Saslav, "Writer-director Cameron Crowe discusses Tom Cruise, newcomer Renee Zellweger, and Hollywood greed," *Industry Central,* http://www.industrycentral.net/director_interviews/CC01.HTM.

"That line has haunted . . . the money.'" Jeff Merron, "Reel Life: 'Jerry Maguire,'" ESPN.com, http://espn.go.com/page2/s/closer/020716.html.

Munchkin

"We had . . . every floor," "They raided . . . armed guards," "They were drunks . . . butterfly nets," "the gulf between . . . people imagined," and "not oversexed . . . undersexed." Aljean Harmetz, *The Making of The Wizard of Oz* (Chicago: Chicago Review Press, 2012), 188, 188, 188, 188, 191.

"sham" and "low-level Munchkin." Stuart Taylor Jr., "Disillusioned 'Munchkin' Strikes Back at 'Wizard,'" *New York Times,* August 26, 1983, A12.

Muppet

"It was really . . . with marionettes." Joel Eisenberg, *Aunt Bessie's How to Survive a Day Job While Pursuing the Creative Life* (Northridge, California: Topos Books, 2005), 63.

"gallery of . . . is founded." Tom Dalzell (senior editor)and Terry Victor (editor), *The New Partridge Dictionary of Slang and Unconventional English, Vol. II, J-Z* (London: Routledge, 2006), 1341.

"'muppet hunt' . . . claims." "Goldman Sachs," *MailOnline (Daily Mail UK),* October 17, 2012, News.

"The point is, ladies and gentlemen, that greed, for lack of a better word, is good"

"Greed is . . . about yourself" and "I never could . . . so many." Bob Greene, "Million Idea: Use Greed for Good," *Chicago Tribune,* December 15, 1986, http://articles.chicagotribune.com/1986-12-15/features/8604030634_1_ivan-boeskys -greed-fund.

"The strangest thing . . . and applause." Stanley Weiser, "Repeat After Me: Greed Is Not Good," *Los Angeles Times,* October 5, 2008, http://articles.latimes .com/2008/oct/05/entertainment/ca-wallstreet5.

"Greed doesn't . . . of fashion." Kurt Soller, "'Wall Street' Screenwriter on the Meaning of Greed," *Newsweek,* March 25, 2009, http://www.newsweek.com/wall -street-screenwriter-meaning-greed-76429.

One-night stand

"only a one-night stand." Mark Twain, *A Connecticut Yankee in King Arthur's Court* (New York: Pocket Books, 2007), 234.

"has been a . . . since at least." Martin Harrison, *The Language of Theatre* (New York: Routledge, 1998), 178.

Oscar-worthy

"Oscar-worthy." Mark Whittington, "Hillary Clinton accuses Bernie Sanders of sexism over 'shouting remark,'" Examiner.com, October 30, 2015, http://www .examiner.com/article/hillary-clinton-accuses-bernie-sanders-of-sexism-over -shouting-remark.

"an Oscar-worthy acting performance." John Shinn, "Sooners' offense unencumbered, execution improved," *Norman Transcript* (Oklahoma), October 18, 2015, Sports.

"Oscar-worthy . . . Platypus Restaurant." Darin Fenger, "First Take: Siri vindicated," *Sun* (Yuma, Arizona), August 22, 2015, http://www.yumasun.com/opinion/ first-take-siri-vindicated/article_77b54d4e-4943-11e5-9130-dfib5a1152c2.html.

Wasps, Beetles, and Lemurs, Oh My! Animals with Celebrity Names

"shameless self-promotion" and "When you . . . have arrived." Untitled, Lisa Merolla, *Popular Mechanics*, September 30, 2009, http://www.popularmechanics .com/science/animals/a4464/4323547/.

"character . . . converted to pastures." Terry L. Erwin, "The Beetle Family Carabidae of Costa Rica: Twenty-nine new species of *Agra Fabricius* 1801 (Coleoptera: Carabidae, Lebiini, Agrina)," *Zootaxa*, December 16, 2002, 36.

Peanut gallery, the

"My dear . . . this theater." "All-Sorts," *Boston Post*, March 30, 1874, 1–2.

Pratfall

"Life becomes . . . and wow!" Ray Bradbury, *Fahrenheit 451: A Novel* (New York: Simon & Schuster Paperbacks, 2013), 53.

Prima donna

"I'm not . . . anyone else." Arianna Huffington, *Maria Callas: The Woman Behind the Legend* (New York: Cooper Square Press, 2002), 168.

"What made . . . her own." "Point and Counterpoint," *Musical America*, July 8, 1916, 26.

"The stuff that dreams are made of"

"was Bogie's idea . . . certainly was." Jeffrey Meyers, *John Huston: Courage and Art* (New York: Crown Archetype, 2011), 75.

"We are such . . . a sleep." Harold C. Goddard, *The Meaning of Shakespeare*, Volume 2 (Chicago: University of Chicago Press, 1951), 291.

Putting on an act

"I'm not . . . the truth." Eleanor Early, "The Shining Talent," *Logansport Press*, Indiana, August 20, 1929, 6.

Quickie

"Hollywood is . . . best players." Louella Parsons, "'Quickies' Latest in Film Production," *The Abilene Reporter-News* (Texas), April 10, 1927, 5.

"There's no place like home"

"No matter . . . like home." Lyman Frank Baum, *The Wonderful World of Oz* (New York: Penguin Books, 1998), 20.

"there's no . . . motif." Aljean Harmetz, *The Making of The Wizard of Oz* (Chicago: Chicago Review Press, 2012), 51.

Ride off into the sunset

"Western addicts . . . faithful mount." Douglas W. Churchill, "Hollywood Gags Up the Fadeout," *New York Times*, October 16, 1938, 161.

"must ride . . . the ranch." Douglas W. Churchill, "'We'll Head 'Em Off at Eagle Pass,'" *New York Times*, April 23, 1939, 108.

"This spirit . . . bat's back." Miles E. C. Sharland (editor), "Prospero and Miranda," *Co-operative News*, September 17, 1898, 1072.

"ride off in the sunset." Josh Alper, "Report: Tom Coughlin to 'ride off in the sunset,'" NBCSports.com, January 3, 2016, http://profootballtalk.nbcsports .com/2016/01/03/report-tom-coughlin-to-ride-off-in-the-sunset/.

Rolling in the aisles

"grew indignant . . . the aisles." "Sunday Delays Call to Trail; I.W.W. Threats and Invitation to London in the Day's Doings," *Trenton Evening Times* (New Jersey), April 14, 1915, 19.

"so marvelous . . . spare us!" *Oxford English Dictionary* (*Aisle* entry), www .OED.com.

"These lads . . . that impropriety." *Illustrated Daily News*, "Plenty of Girls," *Variety*, October 11, 1923, 56.

"I made . . . the aisles." P. G. Wodehouse, *The Most of P.G. Wodehouse* (New York: Scribner, 1988), 631.

"men rolling . . . aisles." Murray Schumach, "Bronx Zoo's Fun-Loving Gazelle Has Men Rolling in the Aisles," *New York Times*, February 4, 1959, 35.

Second act

"there are . . . American lives" and "I once . . . boom days." Audie Cornish, "Fitzgerald Might Disagree With His 'No Second Acts' Line," NPR, May 8, 2013, http://www.npr.org/2013/05/08/182337919/fitzgerald-might-disagree-with-his-no -second-acts-line.

"What we've got here is failure to communicate"

"I thought . . . it perfectly," "I was typing . . . of me," and "it came . . . generation gap." Donald Liebenson, "Frankly, my dear, you can quote 'em," *Los Angeles Times*, January 2, 2010, D1.

"I seem . . . different ways." "Pop Culture 101: Cool Hand Luke," TCM.com, http://www.tcm.com/this-month/article.html?isPreview=&id=355265%7C369667 &name=Cool-Hand-Luke.

"I hated it . . . and unrealistic." Ron Hayes, "Author Has No Failure to Communicate," *Palm Beach Post* (Florida), October 29, 2007, 1A.

Set the stage

"There are . . . third the satiric," "columns . . . to kings," "private dwellings . . . dwellings," and "trees, caverns . . . landscape style." A. M. Nagler, *A Source Book in Theatrical History* (New York: Dover Publications, 1952), 25, 27, 27, 27.

Sixty-four thousand dollar ($64,000) question

"The $64 question." "Anderson, Ind., No. 284," *Typographical Journal*, April 1942, 686.

Smoke and mirrors

"The ability . . . unusual people." *Oxford English Dictionary* (*Smoke and mirrors* entry), www.OED.com.

"Breslin's skill . . . are used . . ." Martin F. Nolan, "The gang that couldn't rule straight, by Jimmy Breslin," *New York Times*, May 11, 1975, BR1.

"Why don't you come up sometime and see me?"

"Every dinner . . . me sometime?" O. O. McIntyre, "Everyday New York," *Orrville Courier-Crescent* (Ohio), December 14, 1933, 6.

Sneak preview

"A sneak . . . shows up." Mark Hellinger, "Goin' to Town with Mark Hellinger," *Lima News* (Ohio), August 5, 1939, 5.

"invention." Idwal Jones, "Lo, the Sneak Preview," *New York Times*, August 4, 1935, X2.

"pioneer." Ed Park, "Freshman Orientation," *Village Voice*, April 12, 2005, http://www.villagevoice.com/film/freshman-orientation-6403899.

"If the screenings . . . directors . . ." Roger Ebert, *Roger Ebert's Movie Yearbook 2004* (Kansas City, Missouri: Andrew McMeel, 2003), 860.

Soap opera

"Fatigue is . . . overtired housewife." "'Soap Opera' Cited as Help to Safety," *New York Times*, October 8, 1947, 19.

"soap opera hams." "Listen! with Slocum," *Washington Post*, December 22, 1939, 32.

"The underlying . . . the sponsor." John Coburn Turner, "'Soap Operas' Are Terrible but Popular," *Washington Post*, May 12, 1940, AM5.

"for listening . . . soap opera." Raymond Chandler, *The Lady in the Lake* (New York: Vintage Books, 1988), 25.

Song and dance

"acrobatic." Edward LeRoy Rice, *Monarchs of Minstrelsy from 'Daddy' Rice to Date* (New York: Kenny Publishing, 1911), 355.

"the greatest . . . the work." "Border Hall—Positively One Night Only!" *Piqua Democrat* (Ohio), April 10, 1867, 3.

Stage Fright

"a fatal . . . success." "Provincial Theatricals," *Morning Post* (London), April 29, 1829, 3.

"sea-sickness." "Recollections of Kean," *National Intelligencer* (Washington D.C.), 2.

"perfectly paralysing." Untitled, *English Gentleman*, May 24, 1845, 78.

"The 'stage-fright' . . . the least." "The Afternoon Playing," *Boston Post*, March 16, 1865, 4.

"Give me . . . to choke." Mark Twain, *The Adventures of Tom Sawyer* (Hartford, Connecticut: American Publishing, 1892), 207.

"Why so serious?"

"one of . . . by Hollywood." Chris Lee, "Bat infiltration; Raising their Internet game, 'Dark Knight' promoters use genre-bending, viral ways to pull in viewers," *Los Angeles Times*, March 24, 2008, E1.

"would you like . . . an accident." Alex Ben Block, "The Dark Knight: anatomy of a hit," *Hollywood Reporter*, August 27, 2008, 7.

Stand-in

"You have . . . the season." Jessica Gardner, "The Pros and Cons, Perks and Demands of Being a Stand-In," *Backstage*, June 16, 2011, http://www.backstage .com/news/the-pros-and-cons-perks-and-demands-of-being-a-stand-in/.

Straight out of central casting

"as though . . . the purpose." "Lucius Beebe: Twelve Years in New York," *Washington Post*, September 21, 1941, L3.

"You can't handle the truth!"

"I just love . . . all night" and "I never . . . of thing." Maeve McDermott, "Watch: Aaron Sorkin discusses his most famous scene," *USA Today*, January 7, 2016, http://www.usatoday.com/story/life/entertainthis/2016/01/07/aaron-sorkin -jimmy-kimmel-jack-nicholson-a-few-good-men/78404018/.

"The character . . . particular individual." William Glaberson, "A Surplus of a 'Few Good Men': Four Lawyers," *New York Times*, September 16, 2011, A18.

Star

"The little . . . abuse him." *Oxford English Dictionary* (*Star*, n., entry), www .OED.com.

"Garrick roused . . . on record . . ." "The Feelings of an Actor, With an Anecdote of Garrick," *Monthly Mirror*, January 1807, 54.

"The word . . . a merciless punster." "Written on the Screen," *New York Times*, November 11, 1917, 80.

"You make . . . a monster." Peter Hay, *Movie Anecdotes* (New York: Oxford University Press, 1990), 69.

"You're a star! . . . a black hole?" Paul F. Boller Jr. and Ronald L. Davis, *Hollywood Anecdotes* (New York: William Morrow and Co., 1987), 436.

Star-studded

"Star-pav'd." John Milton, *Paradise Lost* (London: J. and R. Tonson, 1763), 336.

"Star-inwrought!" Percy Bysshe Shelley, *Beauties of Percy Bysshe Shelley* (London: Stephen Hunt, 1830), 43.

"star-dusted sky." *Oxford English Dictionary* (*Star-studded* entry), www.OED .com.

"Never have . . . of laughs!" Free and Easy (advertisement), *Hamilton Daily News* (Ohio), June 28, 1930, 20.

"There's a star-studded . . . as one." Wm. Nisbet, *Poems* (Chicago: Wm. Nisbet, 1915), 277.

"You know how to whistle, don't you, Steve? You just put your lips together and blow."

"was a scene . . . use it," "When I . . . whistle," and "You are . . . on your face." Todd McCarthy, *Howard Hawks: The Grey Fox of Hollywood* (New York: Grove Press, 1997), Locations 6857, 6857 and 6898 (Kindle version).

Stay tuned

"Emergencies do . . . martial music." Hugh Byas, "Japan, Amid Political Change, Looks Back for a Guidepost," *New York Times*, October 29, 1933, XX2.

"Keyboard Touch . . . hairline precision." General Electric (advertisement), *Washington Post*, September 23, 1938, 11.

"stay tuned . . . broadcast." "More Primary Returns," *Washington Post*, August 9, 1938, X1.

"stay tuned . . . evening." "Tennessee Primary Broadcast," *Washington Post*, August 4, 1938, 1.

"The next . . . stay tuned." Arthur Krock, "In the Nation," *New York Times*, February 22, 1939, 17.

Take a bow

"never 'take . . . that sort." "Star Aerial Performers Are Lin County Residents," *The Cedar Rapids Evening Gazette* (Iowa), March 19, 1913, 3.

"take a bow." "Jimmie Bronson Writes of Boxing Before King and Queen Of Italy," *Joplin News Herald* (Missouri), March 24, 1919, 9.

"You talkin' to me? You talkin' to me? You talkin' to me?"

"Travis speaks . . . mirror." Kevin Jackson, "'There was a sense of exhilaration about what we had done,'" *Guardian* (UK), August 31, 2004, http://www.theguardian.com/film/2004/sep/01/features.extract.

"I'd have . . . different things" and "there were . . . seemed right." Lawrence Grobel, "Playboy interview: Robert De Niro," *Playboy*, January 1, 1989, 69.

"stole that, " "story within . . . story," "true," and "He did . . . talking to me?" Clarence Clemons and Don Reo, *Big Man: Real Life & Tall Tales* (New York: Grand Central Publishing, 2009), 102, 97, 97, 102.

Tearjerker

"America's most . . . inarticulate emotionalism." O. O. McIntyre, "New York Day By Day," *Piqua Daily Call* (Ohio), December 12, 1927, 4.

"tear-jerker . . . love story" and "If I can . . . I'm satisfied." "Tear-Jerker Come-back," *Sun* (Baltimore, Maryland), February 20, 1955, FE9.

That's a wrap

"The British . . . at Bagdad." *Oxford English Dictionary* (*To wrap up* [fig.], entry), www.OED.com.

"At 7:40 . . . this set." Orson Welles and Peter Bogdanovich, *This Is Orson Welles* (Boston: Da Capo Press, 1998), 422.

Thirtysomething

"30-something." Les Barkdull, "Ageless Art [Letter]," *New York Times*, July 26, 1981, A7.

"It wasn't . . . whole conversation" and "The network . . . its name!" Ari Karpel, "Talking About 'Thirtysomething,'" *New York Times*, August 21, 2009, http://www.nytimes.com/2009/08/21/arts/television/21web-thirty.html?_r=0.

"twentysomethings." Robin Abcarian, "Boomer Backlash: Generations: What's it really like to be twentysomething? Douglas Coupland's new novel is a biting portrait of life after yuppiedom," *Los Angeles Times*, June 12, 1991, http://articles.latimes.com/1991-06-12/news/vw-423_1_douglas-coupland.

"fortysomething team." Maureen Dowd, "The Campaign; 2 Baby Boomers on 1 Ticket: A First, but Will It Work?" *New York Times*, July 13, 1992, http://www.nytimes.com/1992/07/13/US/the-campaign-2-baby-boomers-on-1-ticket-a-first-but-will-it-work.html?pagewanted=all.

"You're gonna need a bigger boat"

"Have you . . . broadcasting?" Peter Hay, *Movie Anecdotes* (New York: Oxford University Press, 1990), 22.

"confused." Mark Thompson and Heather Ankeny, "He Wrote *Jaws* and *The Jerk* (with Steve Martin), Carl Gottlieb," www.edge-show.com, April 25, 2013, http://www.edge-show.com/carl-gottlieb-he-wrote-jaws-and-the-jerk-with-steve-martin-collaborated-with-richard-pryor-and-other-greats-and-was-biographer-for-musician-david-crosby/ (approximately 8:40 in the podcast).

"It came . . . very effective." Patrick Jankiewicz, *Just When You Thought It Was Safe: A Jaws Companion* (Duncan, Oklahoma: BearManor Media, 2013).

"You're gonna . . . bigger boat!" Sarah Kent and Cassie Werber, "Gun Ships: Floating Arsenals Battle Pirates on High Seas," *Wall Street Journal*, February 3, 2015, A1.

Top banana

"The average . . . Talking Woman" and "started out . . . Minsky's." Charles D. Rice, "Top Banana . . .," *Sun* (Baltimore, Maryland), December 28, 1947, TW10.

"bladder club." Don B. Wilmeth, *The Language of American Popular Entertainment* (Westport, Connecticut: Greenwood Press, 1981), 16.

"the fruit . . . most desirable." Anthony Slide, *The Encyclopedia of Vaudeville* (Jackson: University Press of Mississippi, 2012), 22.

Typecast

"No, Jimmy Stewart . . . best friend." Ronald Reagan, *Speaking My Mind: Selected Speeches* (New York: Simon & Schuster Paperbacks, 1989), 394.

"Mary Poppins . . . Junkie." George Christy, "Julie Andrews: All the Things I Love Most," *Good Housekeeping*, January 1966, http://www.julieandrewsonline .com/news/1960_news/GH_1966.html.

"If they . . . eight cops." Matt Zoller Seitz, "Why More Actors Should Be Cast Against Type," www.vulture.com, November 4, 2015, http://www.vulture .com/2015/11/actors-should-be-cast-against-type.html.

"Since New York . . . her life." "More or Less in the Limelight," *New York Times*, January 1, 1928, X4.

"Right-to-work . . . public mind," *Oxford English Dictionary* (*Type-cast* entry), www.OED.com.

Well, Isn't That Special? *Saturday Night Live*'s Language Legacy

"It seems . . . personal joke." Tom Shales and James Andrew Miller, *Live from New York* (Boston: Little, Brown and Co., 2002), 323.

Upstage

"'Up-staging' is . . . otherwise have" and "With the chronic . . . prominence." Philip Godfrey, *Back-Stage* (London: George G. Harrap & Co, 1933), 40.

"For all . . . much upstage." J. V. Fitzgerald, "Princeton Ranks in First Flight," *Washington Post*, November 17, 1919, 5.

"Oscar and . . . monkey house." "Finds Blooded Monkey," *New York Times*, April 3, 1926, 3.

Wing it

"projecting wings . . . from abroad." Martin Harrison, *The Language of Theatre* (New York: Routledge, 1998), 309.

"'To wing' . . . a wing." "Wing it," The Phrase Finder, http://www.phrases.org .uk/meanings/412350.html.

"must give . . . play it." Philip Godfrey, *Back-Stage* (London: George G. Harrap & Co, 1933), 39.

"To Wing . . . preparation." *Oxford English Dictionary* (*Wing*, v., entry), www .OED.com.

ACKNOWLEDGMENTS

First and foremost, I must praise my wonderful wife, Jennifer, and my fantastic children, Miller and Becca. I say it with every book I write, but it never gets old: Thank you for your humor, love, patience, and support.

Specific to this volume, there are some folks who deserve to be singled out for credit as well. Much gratitude goes both to my editors at Lyons Press, Rick Rinehart, Stephanie Scott, and Ellen Urban, and my agent, Doug Grad, for making this work possible. I was blessed to get essential advice and input from a group of people who are experts in either writing or show business (and in most cases both): Lionel, Gloria, and Michael Chetwynd, Bob Gale, Alan Gansberg, Jeff Jensen, J. B. Kaufman, Jon Landau, Paula Parisi, Frank Price, Dan Snierson, and Evan Weinstein.

Additional research help was also kindly provided by Rachel Bernstein (Margaret Herrick Library, Academy of Motion Picture Arts and Sciences), Sarah McElroy Mitchell (The Lilly Library, Indiana University, Bloomington), and Steve Wilson (Harry Ransom Center, University of Texas at Austin).

Beyond those who directly helped, I want to give thanks to the various entertainment journalists and showbiz researchers whose work is cited in these pages. This is an industry with a long history of vibrant coverage, and I'm grateful for all the considerable efforts of those on this beat.

A shout-out also goes to Gary Cohen for his logistical assistance.

Finally, I must express my appreciation to Alex Ben Block and Stephen Galloway for giving me my first full-time job covering the entertainment industry at the *Hollywood Reporter*. In particular, Stephen's requirement so many years ago that I vastly improve my film history literacy is hopefully reflected in these pages.

SELECTED SOURCES AND FURTHER READING

Behind the scenes, heaps of research were done to bring you every entry in this book. Many of the resources I relied on can be found in the notes section or the text itself. But in addition, I wanted to highlight a handful of volumes used here that offer a wide scope on either the entertainment business or the language of the industry, or both.

All the Best Lines: An Informal History of the Movies in Quotes, Notes and Anecdotes (2013) by George Tiffin.

A Source Book in Theatrical History: Twenty-Five Centuries of Stage History in More Than 300 Basic Documents and Other Primary Material (1952) by A. M. Nagler.

Back-Stage: A Survey of the Contemporary English Theatre from Behind the Scenes (1933) by Philip Godfrey.

Behind the Scenes: The Making of . . . (1989) by Rudy Behlmer.

Hollywood Anecdotes (1987) by Paul F. Boller Jr. and Ronald L. Davis.

Memo from David O. Selznick (2000) edited by Rudy Behlmer.

Motion Picture Directing: The Facts and Theories of the Newest Art (1922) by Peter Milne.

How Motion Pictures Are Made (1918) by Homer Croy.

I Love It When You Talk Retro: Hoochie Coochie, Double Whammy, Drop a Dime, and the Forgotten Origins of American Speech (2008) by Ralph Keyes.

"It's the Pictures That Got Small" Charles Brackett on Billy Wilder and Hollywood's Golden Age (2015) edited by Anthony Slide.

Motion Picture Handbook: A Guide for Managers and Operators of Motion Picture Theaters (1910) by F. H. Richardson.

*Movie Anec*dotes (1990) by Peter Hay.

Movie Speak: How to Talk Like You Belong on a Film Set (2008) by Tony Brill.

Tales from the Casting Couch (1995) edited by Michael Viner and Terrie Maxine Frankel.

Technique of the Photo Play (1913) by Epes Winthrop Sargent.

Theatrical Anecdotes (1987) by Peter Hay.

The Dictionary of Film Quotations (1995) by Melinda Corey and George Ochoa.

The Fact on File Encyclopedia of Word and Phrase Origins (Fourth Edition) (2008) by Robert Hendrickson.

The Language of American Popular Entertainment (1981) by Don B. Wilmeth.

The Language of Theatre (1998) by Martin Harrison.

INDEX OF IDIOMS, PHRASES, QUOTES, AND WORDS

Below is an alphabetical listing of all the expressions, idiom, quotes, and words that are discussed in this book. Those that are italicized are ones that are mentioned in the text but aren't covered in a full entry.

ABOUT THE AUTHOR

Josh Chetwynd is an award-winning journalist and author. He's covered the entertainment industry for *USA Today* and the *Hollywood Reporter*, twice winning Los Angeles Press Club awards for his efforts on this subject. He's also served as a contributing writer for *Variety*. This is his seventh book, and his second on language, having previously penned *The Field Guide to Sports Metaphors: A Compendium of Competitive Words and Idioms* (2016). Other works include: *How the Hot Dog Found Its Bun: Accidental Discoveries and Unexpected Inspirations That Shape What We Eat and Drink*, which charted on the *New York Times* best-seller list in 2015, and *The Secret History of Balls: The Stories Behind the Things We Love to Catch, Whack, Throw, Kick, Bounce and Bat*, which was named an NPR best book in 2011. He lives in Denver, Colorado, with his wife and two children. Visit www.JoshChetwynd.com.